MW01028837

The MYSTERY *of the Gospel*

Jew and Gentile and the Eternal Purpose of God

The MYSTERY *of the Gospel*

Jew and Gentile and the Eternal Purpose of God

D. Thomas Lancaster

FIRST FRUITS OF ZION

Strengthening the love and appreciation
of the Body of Messiah for the Land,
the People and the Scriptures of Israel

Cover Design:
StudioEMedia.com

First Edition
Printed in the United States of America

Catalog information: Paul & his Writings
CBA Category information: BST, BNT, PAU (Theology)

ISBN: 1-892124-07-6

US Distribution Office
First Fruits of Zion
PO Box 620099
Littleton, Colorado 80162-0099 USA
Phone (303) 933-2119 or (800) 775-4807
Fax (303) 933-0997
www.ffoz.org

Additional Study Resources
Torah Club, a monthly Torah Study Course
HaYesod, a 14 week Hebraic Study Course
Messiah Magazine
Ascend Magazine

Other FFOZ Publications written by D. Thomas Lancaster
Torah Club Volume 4 (see end of book)
Torah Club Volume 5 (see end of book)
Y3K Teaching Seminar, available on DVD or audio CD
Hanukkah and the Disciples of Yeshua

For additonal information, please visit http://www.ffoz.org

To My Noble Wife

אשת חיל

And Soul Companion

Contents

Foreword

Foreword
You Worship the God of Israel

You worship the God of Israel.

We don't often think of it that way, but it is true. The God we worship is the God of the Jews. Edith Schaeffer, wife of the famed Christian intellectual Francis Schaeffer, once published a book titled *Christianity is Jewish.* That title says it all. Our faith is essentially Jewish. Our religion is Jewish. As a believer in Jesus, we are followers of the Jewish Messiah. In Jesus, we are united with the God of Israel.

Within Evangelical Christianity, this is a fact that often goes unnoticed. Our connection to Israel and Judaism is typically overlooked or deliberately ignored. There is an historical and theological disconnect between Christianity and Judaism, between the Church and Israel, between the Law (Torah) and the Gospel. It's as if a spiritual "Berlin Wall" has been erected. There is a partition dividing Old Testament and New Testament, Jew and Gentile. This should not be. God is One, His Word is One, and His people should be One. *Mystery of the Gospel* is about tearing down the dividing wall and rediscovering our common unity.

First Fruits of Zion is a ministry dedicated to strengthening the Body of Messiah's appreciation for the land, the people, and the Scriptures of Israel. Part and parcel of this mission is the restoration of the Written Torah of Moses to believers.

For more than a decade now, First Fruits of Zion has been boldly asserting the eternal validity of God's Holy Torah. Through our materials, Abba has strengthened the hands and hearts of many Jewish believers in and out of the Messianic movement, giving them the confidence to proudly embrace their biblical heritage as part of discipleship to Jesus (Yeshua). However, our ministry is broader in scope than just reaching out to Jewish believers. We maintain that the Torah of God is equally valid and accessible for

Jewish and Gentile believers alike. Torah life is not meant just for Jews; it is meant for all followers of the Jewish Messiah.

In the book of Deuteronomy, God laid out criteria by which Israel was to test religious innovation. He told them that they were to expect a coming Messiah—a "prophet like unto Moses" (Deuteronomy 18:18). But He also warned them regarding future prophets. Deuteronomy 13 provides the criteria: every prophet was to be tested against Moses. If a so-called prophet advocated worshipping another god, or advocated breaking the laws of the Torah, that prophet was a false prophet. Even if he came with signs and wonders, any prophet who led Israel away from God's commandments was not a true prophet at all. He was a false prophet.

If it were true that Jesus was a law-breaker who went about flagrantly violating the Torah and teaching others to do likewise, then we would all be guilty of following a false prophet. Such a Jesus would not even qualify as a prophet, much less the Messiah.

But it is not true. The Jesus of the Bible was a Torah-observant Jew who blamelessly kept the Law of God. Years of anti-Jewish teaching have painted Him otherwise, but the real, biblical portrait of Jesus is not that of a religious revolutionary. He was a Jew, teaching Torah, and living out the Torah as fully expressed in the Kingdom.

To understand how our picture of Jesus became distorted (and how the Jewish and Christian religions became separated) we have to understand something about Jewish history. At the end of the days of the Apostles, there was a great war between Rome and the Jewish people of Israel. The Jews lost. As a result, the Jewish believers also lost. A second revolt a generation later had the same result, coupled with extreme, state-sponsored, religious persecution against Judaism and Torah-living. The surviving believers were mostly people who gave up the Torah. The surviving church was predominantly the Roman church, which only a few centuries later was commandeered by the Emperor Constantine. The rest, as they say, is history.

Almost two thousand years later, we are awakening to our history. Like the orphaned child who is one day told that he is actually the son of a king, we are rediscovering our true, Jewish heritage. As we do, believers from all different denominations and sects are finding common ground. We are coming together with a basis for unity—our common Hebrew Roots.

This was the Master's prayer for us. In John 17:20-21 He prayed, "I pray also for those who will believe in me... that all of them may be one." Ultimately, this unity is accomplished through our common salvation in Jesus. Belief in Jesus is our admission to the family of God. Jesus is at the center of our faith. We share Messiah, we share in His blood, and we share in His empty tomb. Therefore, we are one. Whether we like it or not, we are one body and people.

On another level, however, we can find a basis for unity by acknowledging our common origin. It's not unusual to attend a Bible study where the Torah is being taught and find people who are Catholic, Protestant, Charismatic, Baptist, Lutheran, or any other flavor of Christianity. Our Hebrew heritage, our connection to Israel through Jesus, is something that predates and overrides all of our schisms. It is something all believers share in common. Therefore, it can be a significant basis for unity in the faith. As the foundation of those Hebrew Roots, the Torah is common ground for Gentile believers and Jews alike. It is our deepest root.

Mystery of the Gospel uncovers that common rootedness. The mystery, it turns out, is our shared inheritance in Israel through Messiah. However, D. T. Lancaster goes beyond just pointing out those Hebrew roots. He shows how those roots are at the very center of Paul's proclamation of the Gospel. Lancaster shows us that the Gentile believer's share in Israel is part of the grand scheme of redemption. The Gentile inclusion in Israel is the realization of God's universal Kingdom on Earth. It is profoundly exciting stuff.

This book has evolved significantly over the last two years. We originally intended to publish *Mystery of the Gospel* together with Tim Hegg's *Fellowheirs* in one volume. The authors developed their respective projects in cooperation with each other, and their works share many similarities. What's more, *Mystery of the Gospel* builds primarily upon the careful Bible scholarship of *Fellowheirs,* but develops the material in a different direction. From the reader's perspective, the two books should be regarded as parts one and two of the same project. Both works, however, are strong enough to stand on their own, and ultimately we decided to release them separately.

If you enjoy *Mystery of the Gospel*, you will enjoy the author's other works, *Torah Club* Volumes 4 and 5. Much of the material in *Mystery* is drawn directly from those works. See the Torah Club descriptions on the adjacent page.

I pray that *Mystery of the Gospel* will be an asset to believers everywhere as we all pursue our righteous Messiah and discover our inheritance within the Israel of God. After all, we do all worship the God of Israel.

Boaz Michael
Founder and President
First Fruits of Zion

Other works by D. T. Lancaster

Torah Club Volume Four: The Good News of Messiah

The Gospels! *Torah Club* Volume Four takes students on a passage-by-passage study through the Gospels and the book of Acts. It is a commentary that allows the Gospels to be studied from within the context of Torah and classical Judaism. These materials make the leap and repair the breach between the Torah of Moses and the Gospel of Messiah. Club Members will see Yeshua and His world in vivid new strokes and colors that will fire the heart. Volume Four is eye-opening. It's like reading the Gospels for the very first time.

Torah Club Volume Five: The Rejoicing of the Torah

Standing on the shoulders of Volumes 1–4, *Torah Club* Volume Five incorporates the themes of Torah, Messiah, Prophets, and Gospels laid down in the previous volumes. However, it does not repeat that material. Instead, it rejoins the annual Torah cycle for an exhilarating dance through the narratives, poetry, and laws of the books of Moses, while pulling in relevant material from the Apostolic writings and the epistles of Paul. Questions of practical application are addressed right along with the difficult Pauline passages. Volume Five brings all the Scriptures together in a final celebration of spirit and truth.

The Pilgrimage

Introduction
The Pilgrimage

Blessed are those whose strength is in You,
Who have set their hearts on pilgrimage.
They go from strength to strength,
Till each appears before God in Zion.

—*Psalm 84:5, 7*

To what can the kingdom be compared? It can be compared to a journey—a pilgrimage up to Jerusalem.

Such pilgrimages happened three times a year. For the Holy Festivals of Passover, Pentecost and Tabernacles, all Israel went up to the Temple. The *Mishnah*[1] describes the caravans of pilgrims who gathered in the villages and cities of Israel in preparation for the journey up to Jerusalem. Friends and family, neighbors and countrymen, gathered in the villages of assembly. Final provisions for the journey were purchased. Bags were packed. Prayers for safety were prayed. Overnight the village was transformed into a city of tents. Some slept under the wheeling stars of the open sky. The night passed in anticipation of the journey.

At dawn the head of the assembly awoke the pilgrims by shouting into the early morning air, "Arise, let us go up to Zion, to the House of the LORD our God!" (Jeremiah 31:6). The glad song began.

A flute player led the way. They sang their way to Jerusalem. The miles were many and long, under the sun by day, under the moon by night. Always climbing to higher ground, up into the hill country of Judah. While their caravan traveled, they met other caravans of pilgrims. They joined voices together and continued their song-filled journey. Their feet were weary but their hearts were light. The closer they came to the Holy City, the more crowded the roads became. "Multitudes of people from a multitude of cities flowed in an endless stream to the Holy Temple... from the east and west, from the north and south."[2]

More and more join the pilgrimage to the celebration. As the roads fill with people, distinctions of village, clan and tribe are blurred and quickly forgotten. When at last they lay eyes upon Jerusalem—resplendent, white stone bathed in sunlight—a cheer rises among the travelers. They see the column of smoke rising from the altar to heaven. Before them is the Temple of the LORD.

A pilgrimage to a festival in Jerusalem is a particularly apt metaphor for the People of God. Just as in a pilgrimage, everyone on the road began at a different point of origin, now occupies a different place on the journey, but will one day be joined in one place of glad worship. So too the People of God are comprised of members from many different beginnings, now occupying many different positions on the journey, but ultimately arriving at the same goal. The journey itself is not the goal, but the journey is the means to the goal. Anyone can join the journey, and our joy will not be complete until everyone on the journey has arrived at the destination.

This is a book about the people on the journey. It is not a book about how to join the journey, or why the journey should be made. Those would be topics for other books. Rather, this book deals with the realization that we are not alone on this journey. There are other people on the road. Some of them don't look like us. Some of them do. Some of them seem to be family members; others seem to be strangers from far away. Somehow, we have all been swept up together into something bigger than ourselves. Our individual journeys have been merged into one great movement of people.

That's what this book is about. Some are wondering if perhaps it would not be better for all parties involved if this mass of people were separated into distinct caravans. We could divide it along ethnic lines, or we might divide it along historical religious lines. "Jews should be Jews, Gentiles should be Gentiles." Some have become so enamored of the Jewish pilgrims that they have spurned their own clans and forgotten their own family. "I must be Jewish too," they say. Others have fallen under the impression that differences between the travelers on the road are only superficial and that we are actually all long lost relatives. Many on the journey have demanded that the old family ways be set aside. "Enough with all this glad singing. You Jews must accept the fact that you are Christians now, and we sing a different melody," they say. "After all, this journey is no longer your journey, it is ours."

Recent years have seen significant progress in establishing a biblical basis for Jewish identity in Messiah. The old, unbiblical theologies, which taught that Jews no longer had a place in the Kingdom (short of abandoning Torah and converting to Christianity), have been jettisoned. The Jewish believer in Messiah has come to be recognized as the normal expectation of the Apostolic Scriptures, not the exception to the rule.

Messianic Judaism has rebirthed the phenomenon of "Torah-Christianity," a venture that can only be described as a return to the prototype of biblical faith and observance. This rebirth and return, however, has stopped short of affirming the full participation of both Jews and non-Jews. The prevailing conventional wisdom remains that Jewish believers should do Jewish-Hebraic things (like Torah and Shabbat), while Gentile believers should do Gentile things (like Sunday church and worship).

Those non-Jews who have taken up the call to shoulder the Master's yoke have found themselves trapped in a no-man's land—stuck somewhere between Messianic Judaism (which sometimes only grudgingly offers full participation to other ethnicities) and the mainstream churches (which have not yet acknowledged the continuing relevance of Torah in a believer's life). In short, the message from both parties is that Jews should be Jews and Christians should be Christians.

It is not my intention to suggest that Gentile believers are "Jewish." I understand the term "Jew" or "Jewish" to mean people who trace their family connections to the ancient people of Israel. Neither is it my intention to suggest that Gentile believers should co-opt Jewish culture and tradition. I am a firm believer in the diversity of the body, and it pains me to see Jewish identity eroded by believers who carelessly bandy about Judaica as if those external things were the fullest expression of Torah life. Yet at the same time, to deny Gentiles their full participation in Israel is quite wrong.

As a lifelong Gentile myself, and as a teacher in a Torah community with an 80% Gentile membership, I have been over this ground a few times. This book specifically addresses the position of the Gentile believer within the people of Israel, within the Torah movement of faith, and within the Kingdom of Heaven itself. This is a book about our identity in the People of God.

Yet this book is not a first or final word on the subject. The possibility of Gentile participation in Torah was opened with FFOZ's milestone book *Torah Rediscovered*. That work was followed with the well-reasoned and equally progressive book *Take Hold*. These two excellent works, both still available through FFOZ, laid the groundwork for considering the questions of a Gentile believer's relationship to Torah and Israel.

The broad academic shoulders on which this present book stands is the ruthlessly methodical work of my friend and colleague Tim Hegg. Tim's painstakingly careful research on the place of the Gentile within Ancient Israel provided for me the sure foundation on which to rest the conclusions contained herein. A synopsis of his work was presented in a two-part article published in *Bikurei Tziyon* magazine.[3] That article is currently slated to be released in a book entitled *Fellowheirs*. Tim's work goes a long way toward settling the question of Gentile participation in the community of Torah.

As I began to write, however, I realized that the primary issue at hand is not a question of theological identity as much as it is a question of, "How do I fit into the story?" After all, our Scriptures come to us as a more-or-less continuous, historical narrative detailing the lives and adventures of God's chosen people. The book of Genesis is built on collections of stories, called the *toledot* (genealogies) of the People of God. The *toledot* include family trees containing the details of who begat whom, while also telling the histories of how God interacted with both "Who" and "Whom." For the Jewish believer, these *toledot* are deeply personal because they are the stories of his family, and if he diligently peers into them, he can discern his own place in the sprawling family tree of Jewish and biblical history.

For the Gentile believer, on the other hand, the relationship is not so immediately obvious. We wonder if Abraham is really our father. If so, are Isaac and Jacob also? Is the LORD really "the God of my fathers" or is He "the God of their fathers?" We wonder if we have permission to partake in the Torah. Does our salvation, in one sense or another, make us Jewish? Am I an Israelite?

I hope to answer some of these questions of identity that may haunt Gentile followers of the Jewish Messiah. I expect that Jewish readers will enjoy the book as well, and perhaps even find their own place in the stories in ways they had not previously considered. This book, then, is meant for everyone on the road up to Zion, for everyone on the journey. It is meant for all of us—the First Fruits of Zion.

Next Year in Jerusalem,
D. T. Lancaster

ENDNOTES

1 *Bikkurim* 3:2 The *Mishnah* is the written code of early Jewish legal traditions, sometimes referred to as "The Oral Law."

2 Philo, On Laws 1:96

3 *Bikurei Tziyon* #77, #78. For those who would like to go deeper than the popular level and slog through the Greek, Hebrew and Aramaic, please see Tim Hegg's book *Fellowheirs*, published by First Fruits of Zion.

The Mystery of the Gospel

1

The Mystery of the Gospel

Ephesians

He is an old and worn looking Jew chained to an armed guard. For two years, he has been chained under house arrest while waiting for his trial before Nero. If nothing else, it has given him some time to think. He has had time to mull over the events of his ministry. He has had time to weigh the significance of his amazing journeys and the amazing message of the Gospel he has been proclaiming.

Many of Paul's musings find their best expression in his prison epistles written to the Ephesians and to the Colossians. In those two letters, the Apostle gives us a sense of his own perspective on the Gospel and the consequence of his ministry to the nations. He sums up his life's calling and attempts to illuminate for us the deepest mystery of the Gospel.

In Ephesians chapter six Paul writes, "Pray also for me, that whenever I open my mouth, words may be given me so that I will fearlessly make known the mystery of the Gospel, for which I am an ambassador in chains."[1] What then is the mystery of the Gospel? Why, exactly, is Paul in chains?

Arrest in Jerusalem

One would naturally assume that the "mystery of the Gospel" for which Paul is in chains is the message of Messiah's death and resurrection. After all, that is the good news which Paul proclaimed. One would assume, but one would be wrong.

Paul had been part of the pilgrimage to the festival of Pentecost (Shavuot) in Jerusalem. While in the Temple preparing for the festival he was arrested. His arrest did not come as the result of his preaching the death and resurrection of Yeshua.

Remember that at the time Paul was arrested, James (Yaakov) the brother of the Master was also in Jerusalem preaching the same Gospel, as were thousands of believing Jews, all of them "zealous for the Torah."[2] It would appear that none of them were being arrested, dragged before the Sanhedrin, marched off to Caesarea or sent to Rome.

When the mob of pilgrims was incited against Paul in the Temple, it was not because he was preaching the Gospel. It was not even as a result of his being a believer. At the time of Paul's arrest, the believers were a tolerated, albeit frowned upon, sect of Jerusalem Judaism. So why was Paul attacked by an angry mob in the Temple? The charge leveled against him was that he had brought Gentiles into the Temple. The Acts narrative records the charge against him: "He has brought Greeks into the Temple area and defiled this Holy Place."[3] Luke immediately clarifies for us that the charge is untrue. In verse 29 he writes, "They had previously seen Trophimus the Ephesian in the city with Paul and assumed that Paul had brought him into the Temple area."

Not that Gentiles weren't allowed into the Temple's outer courts. The largest of all the Temple's courts was the great Court of the Gentiles. Men and women from all nations were allowed to ascend to the top of the Temple Mount and congregate in the Court of the Gentiles. There they could worship the God of Israel in His Holy House, a house of prayer for all nations. They could not, however, proceed from the Court of the Gentiles and enter into the Temple proper. A dividing wall stood between the Gentile worshipper and the inner courts of the Temple. Jews were allowed to go in as far as the altar of burnt offering. Gentiles could only look on from a distance.

Josephus writes about the dividing wall of partition, "There was a partition made of stone all around, whose height was three cubits; its construction was very elegant; upon it stood pillars, at equal distances from one another, declaring the law of purity, some in Greek, and some in Roman letters, that 'no foreigner should go within that sanctuary.'"[4] In another place, he says it was "a stone wall for a partition, with an inscription, which forbade any foreigner to go in under pain of death."[5]

In Acts 21, Paul was bringing sacrifices for purification and the completion of a vow. In order to do so, he had to enter the

Temple up to the very Court of Israel. As he was passing from the Court of the Gentiles and into the Courts of Israel, he was seen by several Jews from Asia-Minor. They had earlier seen Paul with Trophimus the Ephesian.

The Jews from Asia-Minor knew Paul. They knew that he was flooding the synagogues all over Asia-Minor with Gentiles, because those were their synagogues. They knew something of his theology regarding Gentiles, if not the details of it. They knew at least enough to be certain that they did not like him. Naturally, they assumed that Paul was bringing Gentiles with him into the Temple area even as he had brought so many Gentiles into their own synagogues. They assumed that Paul was now here in Jerusalem bringing his beloved Gentiles past the dividing wall—into the very Court of Israel!

The ensuing riot was serious enough to elicit a response from the Roman garrison. If not for the quick rescue by soldiers from Fortress Antonia, Paul might not have survived. The commander of the garrison sent troops into the middle of the crowd to pluck Paul out from the fray. They bound him with two chains and tried to ascertain from the crowd exactly what it was that Paul had done, and why it was that everyone wanted to beat the stuffing out of him. The crowd was so heated that the soldiers had to lift Paul up onto their shoulders and carry him back to the fortress. What a scene! Bound with two heavy chains and carried out by soldiers.

When they reached the steps of the fortress, Paul received permission to address the crowd. Hands still bound with heavy chains, he motioned for silence. At last, when his would-be lynchers were quiet, he began to tell his story.

He told them he was a Jew, a Pharisee discipled under Gamaliel. The Gamaliel.[6] He told them his testimony, how he was a persecutor of the believing Jews, how he was on his way to Damascus, how he was blinded and encountered Messiah as a voice from heaven, how he had to be led by the hand to Damascus.

The crowd made no objections to any of these comments. There were no shouts of "Blasphemy!" or jeers at the mention of a voice from heaven belonging to Yeshua. Even the issue of Yeshua's messianic office was met with respectful attention. None of those seemingly controversial claims proved to be the hot button that had raised the mob's ire.

Paul continued his story. He told about how his vision was restored through Chananiah's (Ananias') prayer. He told about his immersion into Yeshua and his return to Jerusalem. He told about praying in the Temple and seeing a vision of Yeshua in the Temple speaking with him. To all of this the crowd still had no objection.

Not until Paul recounted Yeshua saying to him, "Go; I will send you far away to the Gentiles," did the crowd object. This was the hot button.

No sooner does he mention that he was sent to the Gentiles than we read, "The crowd listened to Paul until he said this. Then they raised their voices and shouted, 'Rid the earth of him! He's not fit to live!'" Obviously, Paul's mission to the Gentiles was the issue that triggered the riot. It was not the Gospel of the death, resurrection and messianic office of Yeshua for which Paul was nearly beaten to death and arrested. Rather, it was the message of the inclusion of Gentiles that brought the wrath of Jerusalem onto his head.

The Gentile inclusion in Israel, through the Messiah of Israel, was the real offense of the Gospel to Jewish ears. Paul understood this well. In Galatians 5:11 he made that plain enough by pointing out that if circumcision was a prerequisite to salvation, then "the offense of the cross has been abolished." What is the offense of the cross? It is none other than the Gentile inclusion.

It was for the "offense of the Gospel" (that is, the offensive idea of Gentile inclusion) that Paul had been arrested, tried before the Sanhedrin, marched to Caesarea and subsequently shipped to Rome. Thus when Paul writes that he is an ambassador in chains for the mystery of the Gospel, we are given an important clue to that mystery. Paul was not in chains for preaching Messiah; he was in chains for preaching Gentile inclusion through Messiah. The mystery of the Gospel, for which Paul was in chains, was the Gentile inclusion.[7]

Brothers, Sons of Abraham, and God-Fearing Gentiles

Paul's mission to the Gentiles began to raise trouble for him even before he referred to himself as the Apostle to the Nations. As early as Acts 13, we learn that Paul's inclusive attitude toward Gentiles is going to cause problems. Acts 13 tells the story of Paul and Barnabas attending a synagogue service in the province of Galatia. It was in the city of Pisidian-Antioch. After the reading from the Torah and the Prophets, Paul, the visiting Rabbi from Jerusalem, is invited to present a teaching. Paul stands up and delivers a stirring defense of the Messianic faith in Yeshua. His sermon is well received. The book of Acts tells us, "The people invited them to speak further about these things on the next Sabbath. When the congregation was dismissed, many of the Jews and devout converts to Judaism followed Paul and Barnabas, who talked with them and urged them to continue in the grace of God."[8] Not what we would expect. Here is a synagogue full of Jewish people warmly accepting the message of the Gospel and even inviting the speaker to return the next Sabbath and speak more on the topic.

However, there were others in attendance as well. As Paul began his address he said, "Brothers, Sons of Abraham, and you God-fearing Gentiles, it is to us that this message of salvation has been sent."[9] The threefold address refers to the three types of people one might find in any diaspora synagogue of the first century. These three classes of people have been extensively described in other resources. For now, a brief summary of the three classes will suffice.

1. "Brothers" are Jews: In the context of the Pisidian-Antioch synagogue, Paul's brothers are his fellow Jews. He means to refer to those who are ethnically Jewish, born Jewish as physical descendents of Abraham, Isaac and Jacob. In the first century, "Jew" did not specifically mean someone from the tribe of Judah, but was used as a broad designation to refer to any natural born Israelite. Thus, Paul referred to himself as Jewish, though he was in actuality a Benjamite. The Jews, Paul's brothers, are the Israelites.

2. "Sons of Abraham" are Proselytes: The second type of congregant Paul found in the Pisidian-Antioch synagogue was the proselyte. They were those Gentiles who had for one reason or another decided to make a formal conversion to Judaism under the auspices of the rabbinically prescribed ritual. According to the rabbinic traditions, they were no longer regarded as Gentiles. Through the rituals of circumcision and immersion (and sacrifice when possible), they had been reborn as "Sons of Abraham." This conversion process, as we shall see, was not a biblical procedure as much as a rabbinic contrivance.[10]

3. "God-fearing Gentiles" are Non-Jews: The third type of congregant Paul addressed that day in the Pisidian-Antioch synagogue was the God-fearing Gentile. The term "God-fearing Gentiles" seems to have been used to describe non-Jews who for some reason or another were attracted to Judaism. They worshipped in the synagogue with Jews and proselytes, but chose not to undergo the ritual of conversion. They weren't exactly pagans anymore, but they were certainly not Jews. While they may have been tolerated in the synagogue, and even appreciated for their financial contributions to the community (as with the centurions in Luke 7 and Acts 10), they were not regarded as Jews. They did not enjoy the rights, privileges and responsibilities of Judaism.[11]

As Paul presented the Good News of the Gospel to the Pisidian-Antioch synagogue, he included all three types of people in his address. He declared, "Brothers, children of Abraham, and you God-fearing Gentiles, it is to us that this message of salvation has been sent."[12] His message was well received by the Jews and converts of the synagogue and they invited him to speak again the subsequent Sabbath. As it turned out, however, the God-fearing Gentiles received the message even more enthusiastically. After all, Paul had included them in the Good News. Salvation had been sent to them as well as to the Jews and converts. Through Paul's Gospel, the God-fearing Gentiles could now be regarded as Sons of Abraham, and as Brother Israelites. Word spread rapidly. By the time the next Sabbath arrived, "almost the whole city gathered to hear the word of the LORD."[13]

Offense of the Cross

Almost the whole city gathered? Is that hyperbole? The point is that the synagogue was packed out, standing room only with Gentiles. Not converts. Real Gentiles: *goyim*, *ethnos*, non-Jews… uncircumcised fellows… "Philistines."

From the Evangelical Christian point of view, this would be a happy problem indeed. From the Jewish perspective, however, a Gentile majority in the synagogue was a serious threat to the integrity of the community's identity. Jewish identity was precarious enough in the face of Hellenist society. The mainstream culture was always chipping away at the particulars of Jewish monotheism and Torah observance. A Gentile presence almost certainly would accelerate the tendency toward assimilation. Besides, it was annoying. Jews were, after all, the chosen people. It was their synagogue. Crowding practically every Gentile in the city into the synagogue created both a practical nuisance (Hey, that guy's sitting in my seat!) and a theological conundrum (If everyone is God's Chosen people, then being chosen loses its significance).

Luke tells us, "When the Jews saw the crowds, they were filled with jealousy and talked abusively against what Paul was saying."[14] They were filled with jealousy. They were not jealous because they had never been able to raise such large crowds. (The synagogues were not about the business of trying to bring in big numbers. They were not "evangelical" as we would understand the term.) They were not jealous that Paul and Barnabas had such appeal or that their message seemed to be so popular. They were jealous that the message of the Gospel was compromising the particularity of their theology. The message of the Gospel was throwing the doors of Judaism wide open to the Gentile world. The religion that had previously been a members-only club was suddenly declared open to the public, no table reservations necessary. Paul and Barnabas shrugged off the Jewish objections and continued to teach and minister to the new Gentile believers. But eventually, pressure from the Jewish community forced them out of Pisidian-Antioch.

It is significant that the message of the Gospel itself raised no objections from the Galatian Jewish community. On the contrary, they listened eagerly and wanted to hear more. The message of Messiah's death, burial and resurrection, and the justification and salvation available through Him, sounded good to their ears. They found no offense in the cross. Those were the days before Christian polemics had galvanized Jewish resistance to the Gospel. There was really nothing "un-Jewish" or objectionable about the message of salvation in Yeshua.

Not until they saw the Gentiles crowding into the synagogue did they raise their objections. Not until they realized how this Good News compromised their exclusivity did they reject Paul's message. To the Jewish community of Galatia, the offense of the cross was the inclusion of the Gentiles.

It was a pattern Paul would live to see repeated over and over in city after city. In Thessalonica, the same pattern emerged. Popular success at the synagogue was followed by the conversion of "a large number of God-fearing Greeks and not a few prominent women. But the Jews were jealous..."[15] Everywhere Paul went Gentiles flocked to the synagogue to hear him speak. All over Asia-Minor Paul found Gentiles eager to hear the message of the Gospel and Jews eager to be rid of that same message, not because of theological objections about Yeshua, but because they objected to the inclusion of Gentiles in their faith, religion and synagogue.

It was Jews from these congregations in Asia-Minor who spotted Paul in the Temple in Jerusalem. They were the ones who accused him of bringing Gentiles past the "dividing-wall" and into the Court of Israel, even as he had brought them into their synagogues. They were the ones who instigated the riot and testified against him at his trials. They were the ones responsible for Paul's chains.

The Mystery of Messiah

As Paul wrote the epistle to the Ephesians, the shackles were still on his wrists. He told the Ephesians that it was "the mystery of the Gospel, for which I am an ambassador in chains."[16] He was a prisoner for the sake of the mystery of the Gospel. But what was the mystery of the Gospel to Paul? Why was he in chains? We saw from the story of his arrest in Acts 21 that the mystery of the Gospel which held Paul fast in chains was not the mystery of the death and resurrection of Messiah (though that is very mysterious indeed); it was the mystery of the Gentile inclusion in Israel. To Paul, the inclusion of the Gentiles into the House of Israel was the mysterious part of the Gospel.

He reminds the Ephesian Gentiles that he is a prisoner for their sake:

> For this reason I, Paul, the prisoner of Messiah Yeshua for the sake of you Gentiles—Surely you have heard about the administration of God's grace that was given to me for you, that is, the mystery made known to me by revelation, as I have already written briefly. (Ephesians 3:1–2)

The mystery made known to Paul by revelation was that the Gospel was for Gentiles too. The revelation by which the mystery was made known to him took place in the Temple, many years before, when the Master appeared to Paul in a vision and said to him, "Go; I will send you far away to the Gentiles."[17] Because of that mystery made known to him by revelation, Paul tells us, he is a prisoner for the sake of the Gentiles. Because of that revelation, he was in chains in Rome. He speaks further:

> In reading this, then, you will be able to understand my insight into the mystery of Messiah, which was not made known to men in other generations as it has now been revealed by the Spirit to God's holy apostles and prophets. This mystery is that through the gospel the Gentiles are heirs together with Israel, members together of one body, and sharers together in the promise in Messiah Yeshua. (Ephesians 3:4–6)

What is Paul's big mystery of Messiah? It is that the Gentiles are heirs together with Israel. The Gentiles are together with the Jews as members of one body. The Gentiles share, together with the Jews, the promise in Messiah. That's the big mystery. The Gentile inclusion is the mystery of Messiah.

Such an unanticipated turn of events, from the ethnocentric perspective of Israel, is a mystery indeed! Moreover, it is this mystery, this powerful truth, which inspired Paul's apostleship. It drove him on when all other drives failed. It was the fire that burned in his belly and forced him repeatedly into harm's way. He explains:

> I became a servant of this Gospel by the gift of God's grace given me through the working of his power. Although I am less than the least of all God's people, this grace was given me: to preach to the Gentiles the unsearchable riches of Messiah, and to make plain to everyone the administration of this mystery [i.e. the Gentile inclusion], which for ages past was kept hidden in God, who created all things. (Ephesians 3:7–9)

Clearly, this is deep stuff. Paul is talking about a mystery that has been kept hidden in God for ages. It is a mystery that Paul believes he has somehow been entrusted with. It is a secret concealed for all the ages of creation. "The Gentiles are heirs together with Israel." It is the mystery of Messiah.

ENDNOTES

1 Ephesians 6:19–20

2 Acts 21

3 Acts 21:28

4 *Jewish War* 5:5:2

5 *Antiquities* 15:11:5

6 Gamaliel, Paul's tutor in Torah, is a well known character from Jewish literature. He was a Sage known for his wisdom and piety. In Paul's day, he was the president of the Sanhedrin.

7 Tim Hegg notes that Paul's concept of the Gentile inclusion equaling the Gospel must be what is particularly meant by his peculiar use of the phrase "my gospel" (Romans 2:16; 16:25; 2Timothy 2:8), i.e., the inclusion of the Gentiles as revealed to Paul (as described in Ephesians 3). This also helps explain the term "enemies of the gospel" in Romans. It is not that the people of Israel are enemies of the essence of the gospel (i.e., the means of salvation through God's Messiah). Their aversion to the gospel was a reaction against the inclusion of the Gentiles—which is part and parcel of the gospel message, especially in the teaching of Paul ("my gospel"). Thus, they are not called "enemies of the gospel" but "enemies of the gospel on your account." It is not the gospel, per se, that they are against, but the inclusion of the Gentiles.

8 Acts 13:42–43

9 Acts 13:26

10 See Hegg's work in *Fellowheirs* where he demonstrates that the conversion ritual by which a Gentile becomes "Jewish" is a contrivance of Jewish tradition without warrant in Torah.

11 Ibid.

12 Acts 13:26

13 Acts 13:44

14 Acts 13:45

15 Acts 17:4–5

16 Ephesians 6:19–20

17 Acts 22:21

Sons of Abraham

2
Sons of Abraham
Genesis 12

As Paul began to pore over the Scriptures for confirmation of the mystery he had discovered, he must have rolled the scroll back to the story of Abraham in the book of Genesis. Father Abraham stands as a central figure in Paul's theology. Abraham, who believed God and was credited with righteousness even before circumcision, is a cornerstone of Paul's arguments for the inclusion of the Gentiles.

The story of Abraham begins when he was still called Abram. It begins with a promise regarding his seed and his relationship to the whole world. It begins in Genesis 12 when God says to Abram:

I will make you into a great nation
And I will bless you.
I will make your name great,
And you will be a blessing.
I will bless those who bless you,
And whoever curses you I will curse.
And all peoples on earth will be blessed through you.

The LORD's promises to Abram in this initial covenant oracle culminate with the last line, "All peoples on earth will be blessed through you." It is an astounding promise because of its universal scope. Through a single man, all the families of the peoples on earth will be blessed. God does not say how He intends to accomplish this. He simply assures Abram that, somehow, Abram will be the agent through which all peoples on earth will be blessed.

In its simplest reading, it would seem that we are to understand that all nations will be blessed through Abram—because God has declared that He will bless those who bless Abram. Thus, all nations will be blessed through Abram to the extent that they bother to bless him. If they don't bless him, they won't be blessed through him. It turns out to be good news for Abram because it means that all nations will eventually have to bless him in order for the prophecy of their own blessing through him to be fulfilled. That's a lot of blessing to go around.

As to be expected, the sages of the Talmud and *midrash* were not content with the simple explanation. They saw several deeper meanings in the oracle of Genesis 12. They perceived a way in which Abraham might be a deeper blessing to all peoples.

Procreation or New Creation

The sages take it for granted that Torah is the inspired word of God. That much goes without saying. Furthermore, they teach that every word of Torah is sacred. Even the smallest jot and tittle have meaning. Even the spaces between the letters are important. The choice of a specific word over another word that might have been used is regarded as significant and intentional. Minute details of phrasing and syntax are fraught with meanings. The rabbis' exacting study of such subtle nuances gave rise to the body of interpretation we call *midrash*. *Midrash* means, "something searched out." A *midrash* is an interpretation that has been searched out.

The first words of God's promise to Abraham are, "I will make you a great nation." Those words are loaded with enough nuance and meaning to give rise to a lot of *midrash*. For example, consider the following interpretation.

Reb Berekiah points out that God did not say to Abram, "I will give you a great nation," nor did He say, "I will establish you as a great nation." Rather, it is written, "I will make you a great nation." Reb Berekiah suspects that God must have had a reason for using the verb "make" rather than any of the other possible verbs He could have used. God must have intended to communicate something to us by the deliberate choice of that word. Reb Berekiah suggests that God's choice of words was meant to convey that Abram would become a great nation only after he was remade by God. Reb Berekiah taught that it is as if God said to Abram, "I will make you a great nation, that is after I have created you as a new creation you will be fruitful and multiply."[1]

Reb Berekiah speculates that Abram's metamorphosis into a great nation would not be incumbent upon procreation. Had

God simply meant to prosper Abram into a great nation through the means of fertility and progeny (opening wombs and closing wombs), He might have phrased this blessing otherwise. Instead, God says to Abram, "I will make you." Therefore, in Reb Berekiah's opinion, it was the spiritual rebirth of Abram as a "new creation" that was critical to the fulfillment of the promise. That is why God chose to use the particular verb "I will make you."

Reb Berekiah's interpretation would have fit well with the Apostle Paul's theology. According to Paul, Abraham received the blessings of the covenant on the merit of his faith. Moreover, on the merit of his faith, Abram was remade into Abraham, the father of many nations.[2] For Paul, the story of Abram's transformation into Abraham is the essential prototype of salvation by faith.

In the faith of Abraham, Paul finds a model for the faith of the Gentile believers. By virtue of that same faith which recreated Abram into Abraham, a father of many nations, the Gentiles are also recreated as "new creations."[3] Just as Abram, by faith, became Abraham, a new spiritual creation, so too Gentiles by faith become new creations in Messiah. In fact, the Gentiles who are thus recreated by God are made into sons of Abraham. "So then, [Abraham] is the father of all who believe," Paul writes in Romans 4:11.

By way of this "new creation" through faith, Gentiles are recreated as sons of Abraham. This transaction fulfills the "new creation" name of Abraham, "Father of many nations." Through faith in the God of Abraham, Gentiles from many nations are remade into sons of Abraham. Through the proliferation of these Gentile believers, Abraham has become a great nation, fulfilling the words of the oracle.

It would almost seem that Paul and Reb Berekiah were studying from the same set of notes.

Abraham's Immersion

The sages of the *midrash* kept themselves busy trying to unravel the meaning of the oracle of Genesis 12. In addition to Reb Berekiah's observations about God's choice of a verb in the phrase "I will make you a great nation," the *Midrash Rabbah* goes on to make an issue out of a noun in the phrase "And you will be a blessing." The

Hebrew word for "blessing" sounds similar to the Hebrew word for "pool," and so invites the sages to indulge in some wordplay.

Regarding the clause, "And you will be a blessing," the *midrash* says, "You will be an immersion pool (*berekah*): Just as a pool purifies the unclean, in the same way you bring near to Me those who are far away."[4]

Because the word for "blessing" and the word for "pool of water" are very similar in Hebrew, the sages play off the similar sounding words to construe a new meaning for Abraham's blessing. According to the new meaning, Abraham is to be like a *mikvah* (baptismal pool) which Gentile converts immerse themselves in as part of the rabbinic ritual to become Jewish. Converts to Judaism must pass through a "baptism" in a pool of living water. This immersion into a baptism pool is the final ritual of conversion. Gentiles who pass through the immersion pool are symbolically reborn as Jews (or "born again" as Jews if you prefer). The issues of Gentile conversion, immersion in *mikvah* and being born again will be subjects of a later chapter. For now, suffice it to say that the *midrash* is indulging in some creative wordplay.

It's just a metaphor. Abram isn't really an immersion pool. But how else is one to describe being "baptized" into another except by auspices of metaphor?

In the same way the immersion ritual brings near to God those who were formerly far away (by auspices of conversion), so too Abraham's role is to bring near to God the Gentiles who were formerly far away. By performing this role of bringing the Gentiles near to God, Abraham will be a blessing to the Gentiles. As the pagans embrace the faith of Abraham, they are symbolically immersed into him, as if he was an immersion pool suitable for the conversion ritual.

According to the rabbinic interpretation of the immersion/ conversion ritual, one who immerses in the water undergoes a transformation. He goes down into the water a Gentile, but comes out of it as an Israelite in every regard. Previous ethnic affiliations are no longer deemed relevant, and the new convert is even marriageable for anyone in the Jewish community except the priests.[5]

This *midrashic* re-reading where Abraham is likened to an immersion pool would have suited the Apostle Paul. He uses the same symbolism when he speaks of Messiah. Paul's Gentile converts were "immersed into Messiah Yeshua."[6] Paul employs language similar to that of the *midrash* in order to describe how the Gentiles, who were formerly far away and strangers to the covenants, have now been brought near to God. To the Ephesian assembly he wrote, "Remember that at that time you were separate from Messiah, excluded from citizenship in Israel and foreigners to the covenants of the promise, without hope and without God in the world. But now in Messiah Yeshua you who once were far away have been brought near through the blood of Messiah."[7]

Again, it would seem that Paul was drawing his material from the same sources as the *midrash*. He even employs the same terminology as the sages to refer to non-Israelites: "those far away."

The First Missionary

But how can Abram be compared to an immersion pool? What possible similarity can be construed to exist between Abram and a conversion ritual? Again, we must turn to the sages of the *midrash*. In the *midrashic* commentary on Abraham's life, Abraham is always busy making proselytes from the nations. His goal in life is to spread the knowledge of God and to bring all men to a faith in the One God. Consider my literal, wooden translation of Genesis 12:4–5:

> So Abram went, as the LORD had spoke to him; and Lot went with him. Abram was seventy-five years old when he went forth from Haran. And Abram took Sarai his wife and Lot the son of his brother and all their possessions they possessed and the souls which they had made in Haran, and they went out to go to the land of Canaan, and they came to the land of Canaan.

"The souls which they had made…"? Normally we would smooth out the Hebrew by translating the word "souls" as "people" and the word "made" as "acquired." The sages read the passage literally and object that Abram and Sarai were not able to make souls! What then does the Torah mean by telling us that they made souls in Haran? The literal reading says, "the souls which they had made in Haran."

"Rav Leazar said: 'It refers rather to the proselytes they had made. The verse, as it is written is to teach you that he who brings a Gentile near to God and converts him is as though he had created him.'"[8]

Rav Leazar's explanation of the passage is in accordance with the traditional characterization of Abraham and his relationship to Gentiles. Jewish tradition paints Abraham and Sarah as missionaries for God, actively engaged in the pursuit of the Gentiles. In this manner, Abraham was fulfilling his role as a blessing to all nations. It is by the mechanism of his conversion of the Gentiles to faith in God that Abraham was a blessing and all peoples were blessed through him.

Therefore, just as an immersion pool is the means by which Gentiles convert into Judaism, Abraham was the means by which Gentiles were brought into relationship with the One God. Just as an immersion pool brings near those who were once far away, so too Abraham is the agent which brings the pagan world to a knowledge of God.

In that sense, Abraham was the first missionary.

Blessed and Grafted

In the eyes of the sages, Abraham was to be a blessing to all nations by converting them to faith in God. In support of this view, the traditional sources raise yet another nuance of meaning in the oracle God gave to Abraham.

The Artscroll *Tanach Series Bereishis* commentary cites an opinion regarding the words, "And all peoples on earth will be blessed through you." The opinion states that the verb *v'nivracu*, which means "will be blessed," is related to the *Mishnaic* Hebrew term *mavrik*, which means "to intermingle, to graft." This opinion is based on a grammatical anomaly in Genesis 12:3. The verb "bless" (*barak*) is rarely found in the form (*niphal*) that it appears in Genesis 12:3. The same verbal root, however, is commonly found in this form in regard to "grafting" of plants. Thus, one might translate the verse as "All peoples on earth will be grafted into you."

The context of the passage makes this alternative reading an impossibility. Clearly, the Torah intends us to read, "All peoples on earth will be blessed through you." The passage has nothing to do with the grafting of plants. It is a passage about blessing and being blessed. A responsible translator would never translate the verse to read, "All peoples on earth will be grafted into you."

However, the sages are seldom accused of being responsible translators. In the Talmud, we read the following:

Rabbi Eleazar expounded,

> What is meant by the verse, "And all peoples on earth will be blessed through you."? The Holy One, blessed be He, said to Abraham, "I have two goodly shoots to engraft on you: Ruth the Moabitess and Naamah the Ammonitess." All the families of the earth, even the other families who live on the earth are blessed only for Israel's sake. All the nations of the earth, even the ships that go from Gaul to Spain are blessed only for Israel's sake. (Yavamoth 63a)

Rabbi Eleazar uses the passage to explain how two Gentile women came to be regarded as part of Israel and even mothers of the Davidic kings. Ruth was a Moabite. Naamah was an Ammonite. Regarding Moabites and Ammonites the Torah specifically says, "No Ammonite or Moabite or any of his descendants may enter the assembly of the LORD, even down to the tenth generation."[9] How then could Ruth and Naamah be mothers of the Kings of Israel? Obviously, they were no longer to be considered Moabite and Ammonite. They had been grafted into Abraham.

This creative rereading of the passage is consistent with the above cited *midrashic* interpretations and traditions which portray Abraham as actively involved in missionizing the pagan world. In his efforts to turn the world to faith in God, Abraham could be likened unto a tree of faith. As people leave the pagan religious systems and idolatry of the world, they are like branches removed from trees of other faiths. They are cut from those trees and grafted into the tree of Abraham's faith. Hence, as the peoples of the world turn to faith in the God of Abraham, they are, in a metaphorical sense, engrafted into Abraham. This engrafting process is a blessing to the peoples of the earth, for only in

Abraham's faith can they find truth. Thus, we may read, "all peoples on earth will be blessed through you," as "all peoples on earth will be grafted into you."

Admittedly, the grafting parable is Paul's, but the concept that "all peoples on earth will be grafted into you," is not his invention. Rather, it is an intentional misreading of the Hebrew. Paul and Rabbi Eleazar were virtually contemporaries. Either Paul found the inspiration for his olive tree parable in the same misreading of Genesis 12:3, or both Paul and Rabbi Eleazar shared a common source. At any rate, the imagery is amazingly consistent with Paul's theology.

Paul equates that very line of Hebrew text (Genesis 12:3) with the full message of the Gospel. In Galatians 3:8, he quotes it saying, "The Scripture foresaw that God would justify the Gentiles by faith, and announced the Gospel in advance to Abraham: 'All nations will be blessed through you.'" To Paul, the phrase "All nations will be blessed through you" is the Gospel. In his estimation, those very words are the Good News of Messiah! It is the mystery of the Gospel.

The sages of the *Midrash* understand Abraham's blessing of all nations to be accomplished through the conversion of those nations to faith in God. This is Paul's understanding of the Abrahamic promises as well. In Paul's version of the engrafting parable, Israel is an olive tree and the Gentile believers are olive branches, cut from other trees and grafted into the olive tree of Israel (Romans 11). It is a vivid illustration of the blessing of Abraham to the nations.

All peoples on earth will be grafted into you.

The Seed of Abraham

In Genesis 12 God promised Abram that through him all peoples would be blessed. However, there is a further element to the blessing. In verse seven God promises Abram a seed. He says to Abram, "To your seed I will give this land."

This, of course, was news to Abram, who had no children.

In Genesis 13 God expands upon the seed promise. He says, "I will make your seed like the dust of the earth, so that if anyone could count the dust, then your seed could be counted." Despite these fabulous promises, Abram continued to be childless. As the years went by, it seemed to Abram that God must have overlooked the fact that he had no children.

In Genesis 15 Abram complained to God, pointing out, "Behold, you have given me no seed!" God responded by taking Abram outside on a starry night. He said, "Look up at the heavens and count the stars—if indeed you can count them. So shall your seed be." When God said this to Abram, "Abram believed the LORD, and He credited it to him as righteousness."

God's promise to give Abraham seed was literally fulfilled with the birth of Isaac. Isaac was the seed of Abraham. Therefore, when God tells Abraham to sacrifice Isaac as a burnt offering, it tested both his devotion to God and his faith in the promises of God. When Abraham proved his faith by obeying the horrid command, the LORD rewarded him by reiterating the covenant promises and the promise of his seed. He said, "I will surely bless you and make your seed as numerous as the stars in the sky and as the sand on the seashore. Your seed will take possession of the cities of their enemies, and in your seed all nations on earth will be blessed, because you have obeyed me."[10]

Notice how the promise has expanded in this passage. The original covenant blessings of Genesis 12 have been combined with the seed promises of the rest of the Abrahamic narrative. Most significant is that the key text from Genesis 12, "all peoples will be blessed through you," has now been specified to say, "in your seed all nations on earth will be blessed."

The *midrash* on Genesis 12 understands the promise of "all peoples being blessed" to mean that through Abraham all peoples would come to faith in God. In Genesis 22, this promise has been transferred to Abraham's seed, Isaac. Through Isaac, all nations on earth will be blessed. Through Isaac, all nations will come to faith in God.

This idea is repeated in Genesis 26:4, where God passes the blessing to Isaac saying, "in your seed all nations on earth will be blessed." From Isaac the promise is passed to his seed Jacob to whom God says again in 28:14, "All families on earth will be blessed in you and in your seed."

Let's consider this for a moment though. How is it that Abraham's seed is to be the vehicle by which all nations might be blessed? How is it that through Abraham's seed all nations should come to faith? Paul comments on these questions in Galatians 3:16. In that passage, Paul points out that the Seed of Abraham and the seed of the patriarchs is always represented in the Hebrew by the singular form of the noun. Paul says, "The promises were spoken to Abraham and to his seed. The Scripture does not say 'and to seeds,' meaning many people, but 'and to your seed,' meaning one person, who is Messiah."[11]

According to Paul, the promised Seed of Abraham is not a multitude of nations, nor is it a vast sea of people. Rather, it is a singular individual by whom vast seas of people are blessed, and multitudes are recreated as seed of Abraham.

For Paul, the promise of the seed finds its ultimate fulfillment in Messiah, a singular seed of Abraham. This singular seed is the agent through which all peoples and all nations are blessed (converted). He is the seed through which the Gentiles are made into new creations. He is the seed through which those far off are brought near. He is the seed into which the unclean are immersed and made clean. He is the seed by which the wild olive branches are grafted into the family tree of Israel.

Through the work of the singular seed of Abraham, Gentiles from all nations are to be transformed into the uncountable seed of the promise. He concludes his argument at the end of chapter three when he declares to the Gentile Galatians, "You are all sons of God through faith in Messiah Yeshua, for all of you who were baptized into Messiah have clothed yourselves with Messiah. There is neither Jew nor Greek, slave nor free, male nor female, for you are all one in Messiah Yeshua. If you belong to Messiah, then you are Abraham's seed, and heirs according to the promise."[12]

According to Paul, if we belong to Messiah (who is the Seed of Abraham) then we are Abraham's seed and the recipients of the promise to be blessed in that seed. The scriptural criteria for determining if one is indeed of the "Seed of Abraham" is not genetic, it is spiritual. If you belong to Messiah, then you are Abraham's seed, and an heir according to the promise.

All Peoples on Earth Will be Grafted into You

We saw how an "alternative" reading of the Hebrew of Genesis 12:3 could be construed to read, "All peoples on earth will be grafted into you."

Paul seems to have taken his cue from the same "alternative" reading, but even if he did not, he somehow came to the same conclusion. In Romans chapter 11, he spelled those conclusions out in no uncertain terms.

In that passage, he compares Israel to an olive tree. Regarding the olive tree of Israel, he writes to his Gentile readers in Rome that they have been adopted into the family tree of Israel. They are adopted like wild olive branches taken from other olive trees (other nations) and grafted into the olive tree of Israel. The result of the engrafting is that they have become a full part of the olive tree of Israel. They are no longer Gentiles in the strict sense. In Messiah, there is neither Jew nor Greek. Instead, both the natural descendents of Abraham and the spiritual descendents comprise the common entity of Israel.

In this sustained metaphor for spiritual adoption, Paul warns the Gentiles not to become arrogant over the natural branches. Rather, they should remember that as engrafted branches, they are the guests. He admits that some of the natural branches have been removed from the tree because of their unbelief. However, even this unbelief he explains away as a necessary and temporary state to allow time for the nations to come to faith.

Who are the natural branches that have been removed? The context of the book of Romans seems to make it clear that those branches are Paul's own Jewish contemporaries who have rejected the Gospel. Regarding those branches, Paul tells us, "As far as the Gospel is concerned, they are enemies on your account; but as far as election is concerned, they are loved on account of the patriarchs, for God's gifts and His call are irrevocable." In other words, don't be too quick to count them out.

In Romans 11:25 he says, "I do not want you to be ignorant of this mystery, brothers, so that you may not be conceited: Israel has experienced a hardening in part until the fullness of the Gentiles has come in."

But the point is simple. If you belong to Messiah, then you are Abraham's seed, and heirs according to the promise. The only criterion is belonging to Messiah.

ENDNOTES

1 *Bereishit Rabbah* 39:11

2 Romans 4:16, 17

3 Galatians 6:15

4 *Bereishit Rabbah* 29:11

5 Those of priestly descent.

6 Romans 6:3

7 Ephesians 2:12,13

8 *Torah Temimah* cited in Artscroll's *Bereishis* 435

9 Deuteronomy 23:3

10 Genesis 22:17,18

11 Tim Hegg points out that Paul's grammatical point is itself a *midrash*. The Hebrew *zerah* (seed) is a collective singular (its one plural form, 1 Sam 8:15 is an anomaly). Paul must be making a *midrash* on the grammatical fact that *zerah* is a collective singular.

12 Galatians 3:26–29

The House of Joseph

3
The House of Joseph
Genesis 45

Stories are powerful—As Paul wrestled through the mystery of the Gospel, trying to come to terms with the Gentile inclusion, he must have rolled the scroll to the stories of Joseph. Voices other than Paul's were already retelling the stories of Joseph as metaphors for Gentile inclusion... and exclusion.

The Torah tells a story about Joseph taking a wife in Egypt. It tells us that during Joseph's time of estrangement from his family, he took an Egyptian bride. Her name was Asenath. She was the daughter of a pagan priest.

We are told nothing else about her except that she bore Joseph two sons, Ephraim and Manasseh. Her two sons later go on to be patriarchs of two of the Twelve Tribes of Israel.

Joseph's Egyptian wife is something of an embarrassment to the sages. Abraham's wife Sarah was a Hebrew like himself. When Abraham sought a wife for his son Isaac, he sent his servant on a quest to his own people. He wanted a Hebrew Shemite bride for his son. Abraham's servant procured Rebecca. Isaac and Rebecca had two sons. They grieved over Esau because he took wives from among the local girls. Jacob's wives, on the other hand, were Hebrew Shemites like his mother and grandmother. But this Asenath was the daughter of an Egyptian priest, and hence a Hamite. Joseph's marriage to her appears to be a breach of ethnic fealty. One can almost hear Grandma Rebecca's disapproving "tsk tsk" echoing from inside the Machphelah tomb in Hebron.

Daughter of Dinah

The embarrassment over Asenath comes from the implication that two of the Israelite tribes now have Egyptian blood in their veins. In response to this uncomfortable moment in the Torah, the sages supply a *midrashic* explanation for Joseph's marriage to Asenath. The *midrash* would have us believe that Asenath, unbeknownst to Joseph, is actually his niece, the daughter of his sister Dinah. Through miraculous circumstances, Asenath was adopted by Potiphera and raised as an Egyptian. Therefore, Asenath, the bride of Joseph was actually not an Egyptian at all. She was really an Israelite in disguise. The happy result of this retelling of the story is that Ephraim and Manasseh (and hence the tribes that bear their names) are then full-blooded sons of Jacob.

The *midrash* we are speaking of says, "When Shechem son of Hamor violated Dinah, she conceived and bore Asenath. Jacob's sons wished to kill the child. What did Jacob do? He inscribed the Divine Name on a gold foil, hung it about her neck, and sent her away. The angel Michael descended and brought her down to Egypt into the house of Potiphar. Potiphar's wife, being barren, raised Asenath as a daughter." [1]

In the *midrash* Jacob's gold foil tag with the ineffable Name inscribed on it serves to identify her later. This assures us that she is indeed Dinah's daughter and not a horrid Egyptian woman at all. A sigh of relief is heard in Hebron.

The *midrashic* revision of the story is primarily concerned with the purity of bloodlines. We can imagine the sage who created this explanation for Asenath. He is a respected teacher in his community, perhaps with his own school of disciples. As the Torah authority of the local *Beit Midrash* and synagogue, he feels responsible for safeguarding the community. What's more, he is not particularly fond of proselytes.

He has seen both converts to Judaism and Christians turn against Jews when the political pressure to do so was applied. He has seen the deleterious effects of the Greek worldview on the Torah community. He has had to deal with the halachic problems raised by mixed marriages. He has seen more than enough Jewish blood spilled by Gentile hands.

His disciples come to him with a question. "Master," they ask, "How is it that Joseph, who proved his purity and devotion to his father's family when tempted by the Egyptian woman, succumbed to be married to the heathen daughter of an Egyptian priest?"

The old sage considers the question. How should he answer? He might answer, "Asenath was a proselyte that converted to Judaism, thus Joseph was free to marry her." But such an answer would seem to sanction mixed marriages. It might even encourage his disciples to consider Gentile women, Heaven forfend. What would prevent them from marrying Gentile women whom they might convince to make a similar conversion? Furthermore, such an answer would imply that the tribes of Ephraim and Manasseh were not pure descendents of Shem. It would be an unconscionable conclusion to reach. The Sage understands that his telling of the story of Asenath will shape the identity of the Jewish community for better or for worse.

He considers it a moment more and answers with a question, "What of the other eleven brothers? From where did they obtain their wives?"

His disciples have no answer. This question had not previously occurred to them. From where indeed? Aside from Judah, the Torah does not say.

"I will tell you from where," the sage says. "The wives of all the Tribes were born along with them, from the same womb even. Each of Jacob's sons was born as a fraternal twin with his wife. Thus, God provided good Israelite wives for each of our fathers. Except for Joseph."

Now the sage has a smile on his face. He has his disciples hanging on his every word. Their mouths are agape. Their eyes are riveted on him. He chuckles as he asks, "And from where was Joseph to obtain a wife? Why did God provide an Israelite bride for each of his brothers but not for him?"

The disciples shake their heads. They do not know why.

"I'll tell you why," the sage says. "Because Dinah's daughter Asenath was fitting for him as a wife."[2] As his explanation grows, the story of Asenath's birth, her abandonment, her angelic transportation to Egypt and her adoption by Potiphera are all supplied as necessary details to support the premise.

By imagining sibling-spouses for the sons of Jacob and by reinventing Asenath as a granddaughter of Jacob, our sage has avoided the unpleasant implications of mixed bloodlines. In addition, he has protected his ethnocentric worldview, which places Gentiles outside of the People of God. Never mind that Dinah's own daughter, daughter of a Canaanite rape, could hardly have been of pure bloodlines herself. It is enough that the reproach of Joseph has been removed.

He has reinvented Asenath. He has made her into a symbol and confirmation of the exclusion of the Gentiles. She may at first appear to be a Gentile convert, but on closer examination, she proves to actually be a lost daughter of Israel. Objections to his interpretation are waved away by fanciful claims and a creative retelling of the story. Asenath must be Israelite, because the alternative is unthinkable. It cannot be proven and it need not be proven, because it is a matter of identity. It is a story, not a history.

However, his fanciful retelling is contrary to the literal reading of the Torah. In the Torah account Asenath is Egyptian. She is the blood-daughter of an Egyptian, and Joseph marries her because he has no hope of ever being reunited with his family. His marriage to her results in two sons. Joseph names the eldest Manasseh (Forgetful) because he has forgotten his father's family. He names the second son Ephraim (Doubly-Fruitful) because God has made him twice fruitful with two sons.

The *midrash* wants to adjust the plain meaning of the text in order to avoid the unpleasant implication that two of the tribes of Israel have an Egyptian mother. By trying to control the story, the *midrash* hopes to control Jewish identity.

Daughter of Egypt

But there is another and perhaps older answer to the question his disciples posed. There is another interpretation of the Asenath character. This interpretation comes from the pen of a Greek-speaking Jewish author living sometime in the first century of the Common Era. We don't know his name or where he came from, but we can infer some things about him from his writing. He wrote in Greek. He had an interest in things Egyptian and seemed to have firsthand knowledge of Egyptian geography. He may have been an Egyptian Jew living in Alexandria.[3]

In his community, he had probably seen scores of Gentiles turn from their pagan worship systems and attach themselves to the God of Abraham. The great port city of Alexandria afforded him plenty of occasions to rub shoulders with all manner of men. He met people from all nations who had joined themselves to Israel as proselytes and converts. They were Greek speakers for the most part, but they possessed a deep passion for the God of the Hebrews. They were God-fearers, converts and Christians.

They crowded themselves into the Great Synagogue; they pressed themselves in among Israel. From the Egyptian writer's perspective, the presence of those Gentiles enriched the family of God.

As a result, he took a very positive view of converts. It is possible that he himself was a convert to Judaism. In his book, *Joseph and Asenath*, his interpretation of the Asenath character is considerably friendlier toward Gentiles than that of the *midrash* cited above. The story is written in Greek, but it is Jewish to the core. It is a suggestively erotic love story between Joseph and his Egyptian bride.

In the story, Asenath is portrayed as a breathtakingly beautiful, virgin daughter of an Egyptian priest. Despite her great beauty, she is completely devoted to idolatry and worships all the gods of Egypt. Yet, when she lays eyes on Joseph, she is smitten with him. She is so smitten that she says, "I did not know that Joseph is a son of God."[4]

She tries to woo him, but he is not interested. He rebukes her for her idolatry, and she is filled with shame. Having fallen utterly in love with Joseph, she destroys all of her idols, repents for seven days in sackcloth and ashes, and calls upon the God of Joseph.

During her seven days of repentance, a heavenly man appears to her. He is described as "a man in every respect similar to Joseph... except that his face was like lightning and his eyes like sunshine and the hairs of his head like a flame of fire of a burning torch, and hands and feet like iron shining forth from a fire..."[5] The heavenly Joseph-Man is similar to the Son of Man descriptions in the books of Daniel and Enoch.

The Joseph-Man speaks to Asenath saying,

> Take courage, for behold your name was written in the book of the living in heaven in the beginning of the book, as the very first of all, your name was written by my finger and it will not be erased forever. Behold, from today, you will be renewed and formed anew and made alive again and you will eat the blessed bread of life, and drink a blessed cup of immortality, and anoint yourself with blessed ointment of incorruptibility. And your name shall no longer be called Asenath, but your name shall be City of Refuge, because

> in you many nations will take refuge with the LORD God, the Most High, and under your wings many peoples will be sheltered and behind your walls will be guarded those who attach themselves to the Most High God in the name of repentance.[6]

Asenath's encounter with the divine Joseph-Man is followed by her conversion into a worshipper of the LORD God, Most High. She confesses her sins and washes herself from the ashes of her repentance. She dresses herself in a wedding garment and waits for her beloved to return.

The Pharaoh of Egypt informs her, "The LORD, the God of Joseph, has chosen you as a bride for Joseph, because he is the firstborn son of God. And you shall be called a daughter of the Most High."[7]

At last, Joseph and Asenath are married, after which Asenath says to Joseph, "Your father Israel is like a father to me."

City of Refuge

Joseph and Asenath is an important work because it presents a first century typology of both the Joseph character and the Asenath character. In the mind of the writer of *Joseph and Asenath*, Joseph represents a Messiah character. He is even called "the firstborn son of God." The Divine Joseph-Man gives Asenath to eat from the "blessed bread of life" and to drink from the "blessed cup of immortality." These are clear allusions to the rites of the Pesach communion. It is through the agency of this Messianic Joseph character (who is represented as both divine and earthly) that Asenath is converted from paganism to the worship of the one true God.

The imagery seems pointedly Christian, and it may be that our Alexandrian Jewish author was also a believer.[8] The majority of critics maintain that *Joseph and Asenath* is a Jewish work, too Jewish to be written by a Christian. But the rigid distinction we assume between Judaism and Christianity did not exist through most of the first century. It is completely possible that the author of *Joseph and Asenath* was a Jewish believer.

Unlike the *midrashic* explanation of Asenath, our unknown author revels in Asenath's Gentile roots and pagan origin. It is precisely her Gentile and pagan nature that intrigues him. In her, he sees a model for all future converts to Judaism. She is a "City of Refuge" for all nations and peoples who attach themselves to the Most High God.

In creating this charming story, our unknown Jewish author lends us an important, alternative interpretation to the Asenath character and the Gentile question. His readership was probably composed of Gentile converts to Judaism (or the sect of Judaism called "The Way"). Asenath is offered to them as a sort of "patron saint." She is the Torah matriarch for Gentiles seeking legitimacy in Israel.

In this respect, Asenath's character is a proto-Ruth. Like Ruth, Asenath is a Gentile daughter of a people forbidden to intermarry with Israel. Like Ruth, Asenath makes a dramatic declaration of conversion. Like Ruth, Asenath is ultimately brought into Israel through marriage to a Redeemer-Messiah character.

Through her attachment to Joseph, she becomes the bride of a Son of God and a daughter of the Most High.

Will the Real Asenath Please Stand Up

These two interpretations of Asenath are roughly contemporary. Yet they could not be more opposite in orientation. The *midrashic* view rises from a defensive and ethnocentric Judaism which views Gentile converts as a threat to the integrity of Jewish race and religion. The Joseph and Asenath view rises from a confident and expansive Judaism which views Gentile converts as a compliment to Israel and a testimony to the universal validity of faith in the One God.

Which view is correct? It depends on who you ask.

Neither story is actually historical. Rather, they are stories written to shape a people's corporate self-consciousness. Whoever controls the stories of a people controls the identity of the people.

The two versions of Asenath have striking similarities to the questions posed by many non-Jewish believers in the Hebrew Roots and Messianic movements today. Which Asenath better represents Gentile believers? Are we like the daughter of Dinah, lost and forgotten Israelites raised in a Gentile environment, ignorant of our own true identity as Israel, until it is revealed to us through our salvation? Or are we like the daughter of the Egyptian priest, fallen head-over-heels in love with Joseph the Israelite, forsaking our pagan identity and clinging to him and his God?

It depends on who you ask, but the author of *Joseph and Asenath* definitely would place us in the latter camp. His Messianic treatment of Joseph creates a typology into which Yeshua fits very well. As the bride of Yeshua, we are His Asenath. And like Asenath, we are brought into the family of Israel through our husband. As Asenath tells Joseph in the story, "Your father Israel is like a father to me."

Asenath is a City of Refuge in Israel for those of us who have attached ourselves to the Most High God, the God of Israel.

A Prayer for Asenath

In the story *Joseph and Asenath*, Joseph prays for his beautiful Egyptian princess prior to her conversion.[9] It eloquently expresses the hope of our faith, our desire to be born again, to be remade and renewed and brought into the family of the God of Israel.

Listen to the words of Joseph as he prays for his Gentile bride.

LORD God of my father Israel
The Most High, the Powerful One of Jacob
Who gave life to all
And called from the darkness to the light
And from the error to the truth
And from the death to the life.

May You, LORD, bless this virgin,
And renew her by your spirit,
And form her anew by your hidden hand,
And make her alive again by your life,
And drink your cup of blessing,
And number her among your people
that you have chosen before all came into being,
And let her enter your rest
which you have prepared for your chosen ones,
And live in your eternal life forever and ever.

ENDNOTES

1 *Midrash Aggadah, Bereishit* 41:45. See also *Yalkut Shimoni, Vayishlach* 134. Both cited by Chasidsah, 1994.

2 *Pirkei d'Rabbi Eliezer* 36

3 See Burchard's introduction to *Joseph and Asenath.* Charlesworth (1983).

4 *Joseph and Asenath* 6:5

5 *Joseph and Asenath* 14:9

6 *Joseph and Asenath* 15:2–7

7 *Joseph and Asenath* 21:4

8 However, Burchard's introduction to the work claims that "every competent scholar has confirmed that *Joseph and Asenath* is Jewish." (Page 186 Vol. 2. Charlesworth, 1983).

9 *Joseph and Asenath* 8:9

Joseph and His Brothers

4
Joseph and His Brothers
Genesis 45

Almost a decade later, Joseph found himself face to face with his long-estranged brothers. When at last he could control himself no longer, he turned his back on his guests and servants and shouted in Egyptian, "Have everyone leave my presence!"

Only Joseph's stunned and terrified brothers were left. Judah was still on his knees in front of the Egyptian governor, but the governor had turned his back. There was absolutely no sound at all. Judah let his eyes travel across the abandoned hall. He looked into the wide-eyed and terror-stricken faces of his brothers.

Suddenly there was a sound from the governor. It was a small gasp, a breath, a sob. His shoulders convulsed as another, deeper sob escaped from his body. And then another sob followed by another one, rising from deep inside of him, and the governor sank to the ground, his back still turned away from the anxious brothers. His sobs broke into a wailing howl of such immense sorrow and pain that Judah felt his own eyes fill with tears, despite himself.

The Egyptian governor turned toward the brothers, tried to stand, but the weight of his agonized weeping buckled his knees and he stumbled to the ground again.

The brothers stared, uncomprehending. They began to suspect that they had fallen victim to a lunatic. But this lunatic was reaching out his hand toward them, beckoning. Only by great force of will was he able to choke out two simple Hebrew words between his cries. He said, "*Ani Yoseif.*"

To the brothers, he may as well have still been speaking Egyptian, because even in their own language, the words he spoke to them now made no more sense than the Egyptian words had. He said, "I am Joseph. Is my father still living?"

Who is Joseph?

Stories are powerful, and few are more powerful than this one.

The scene in which Joseph reveals his identity to his brothers is the climactic moment of the book of Genesis. Everything in the narratives of Genesis builds to that point. All the stories of the patriarchs culminate in chapter 45. The Joseph story itself is the longest continuous narrative of the entire Torah. The Joseph chapters are the highest drama of Genesis, and chapter 45 is the highest point of drama in those chapters. If Genesis is a symphony of emotion and meaning, it has reached a crescendo, and every instrument has been called into play. With all of Genesis pointing to this moment, it could be that God intends to communicate something to us here.

To truly enter into the moment, we must remember that at this point in the story, Joseph's brothers still have no idea who he is. Joseph is dressed like an Egyptian. He has Egyptian hair and Egyptian makeup. He speaks the Egyptian language, and until this moment has only spoken Hebrew through a translator. To the eleven brothers, Joseph is a Gentile prince. They have no idea that this is their own brother, the one sent to them by their father so long ago, the one they rejected, stripped, put into the earth, and gave over to the Gentiles. And how could they suspect it? The brothers had long ago come to regard Joseph as dead, convincing themselves of their own deceit to explain his absence. To the brothers, there is no Joseph.

Ever since the days of the Master, His followers and believers have explained the importance of the Joseph story as a type and foreshadowing of the story of Yeshua. Although the Apostolic writers never directly invoke Joseph as a typological prophecy of Messiah, the symbolism is unavoidable and remarkably clear. The line of connection between Joseph and Yeshua was certainly not lost on the Christian readers of *Joseph and Asenath*. In that work, Joseph is the firstborn Son of God, manifested in both a human and a divinely glorified state, offering his bride to eat from the blessed bread of life and to drink from the blessed cup of immortality.

So while we read the story of Joseph, we must remind ourselves that there is another story at work here, the story behind the story, a deeper meaning, a Messianic *midrash*. It runs parallel to the Joseph story like a second line of narrative. It is the deep mystery of Genesis. It is the story of our Master and His reconciliation with His brothers.[1]

Yeshua, like Joseph, was sent to His brothers, the people of Israel. Like Joseph, He was sent by His father. Like Joseph, His brothers did not receive Him. Instead, He was rejected, stripped, killed, put into the earth and ultimately given over to the Gentiles.

Like Joseph, Yeshua was variously received among the Gentiles, but eventually rose to an unparalleled position of prominence in the Gentile world. Like Joseph, He became the agent for the salvation of all nations. And like Joseph, He was all but forgotten by His own true brothers.

Just as Joseph was 'disguised'—made unrecognizable by his Egyptian clothing and hairstyle, so too has the Messiah been made unrecognizable—'disguised' by Gentile culture. We have painted Him to look like one of us. We have represented Him in our artwork with Gentile hair, makeup and clothes. We have made His mouth speak in Greek and in the language of every nation, but we have forgotten that He spoke Hebrew first. We have removed Him from His Hebraic and Torah context, and made Him unrecognizable to His own brothers. Historically, the harder we have tried to convince Jews otherwise, we have only strengthened their conviction that this Jesus is not a Jew, and He is certainly not their Messiah.

The Christian inclination is to exclaim in frustration, "Look, He's really Joseph, your brother! Look, can't you see it? Here, read this! I've written a book on it!" Our efforts are of little avail. From the brothers' perspective, we are speaking Egyptian. We are pointing to an Egyptian.

When Joseph finally chooses to reveal his identity, it is in his own timing and his own venue. He clears the room of Gentiles. There is nothing for any of the Egyptian court to contribute or to add to the moment. It is only theirs to hurry and get out of the way. So too with us from the nations. When the Master chooses to reveal Himself to His brothers, it is He who does the revealing. That much is certain.

The great Chassidic teacher Reb Meir Yisrael, better known as the Chofetz Chaim, commented on this very passage of Genesis.

Like so many others before him, he intuitively sensed the great import of the events being described as Joseph revealed his identity to his brothers. Regarding this moment in Torah, Reb Yisrael said the following:

"When Joseph said, 'I am Joseph,' God's master plan became clear to the brothers. They had no more questions. Everything that had happened for the last twenty-two years fell into perspective. So, too, will it be in the time to come when God will reveal Himself and announce, 'I am the LORD.' The veil will be lifted from our eyes and we will comprehend everything that transpired throughout history."[2]

The Chofetz Chaim was not a believer in Yeshua, but his words penetrate directly to the heart of the matter at hand. What more is there to say? The veil is lifted. This is the climax of the story, the culmination of events, the crescendo of the symphony! Everything has been building to this moment. It is that long awaited moment when Messiah Himself lifts the veil and reveals Himself to His brothers saying, "*Ani Yeshua*! I am Yeshua, your brother."

"Then the veil will be lifted from our eyes and we will comprehend everything that transpired throughout history."

That moment will happen. In the book of Romans, Paul declares with absolute confidence, "All Israel will be saved."

Joseph's Shadow

In the Torah, when Joseph revealed himself to his brothers, he said, "'Come close to me.' When they had done so, he said, 'I am your brother Joseph, the one you sold into Egypt! And now, do not be distressed and do not be angry with yourselves for selling me here, because it was to save lives that God sent me ahead of you.'"[3]

Joseph tells his brothers not to be angry or regretful over the circumstances of the past. It was God's plan that he should be estranged from them. It was God's plan to send Joseph ahead of them to save lives. Joseph uses the same Hebrew word that is used for resurrection from the dead, *l'michyeh*.

So too Yeshua's rejection by Israel has meant wealth for all nations. His rejection at the hands of His brothers was a central part of God's eternal plan to bring salvation and resurrection to all peoples, even to His own brethren.

Christians always ask, "If Jesus fulfilled the Old Testament prophecies so perfectly, why couldn't the Jewish people see it? Why did they reject Him?" The answer is simple. They rejected Him because God willed it. And God willed it to save lives. God sent Him ahead of His brothers to save lives.

The book of Romans tells us of a hardening. Corinthians tells us of a veil. We live in the days that the Apostolic Scriptures call the time of the Gentiles. Paul tells us, "The Jewish rejection meant riches for the world!"[4] So too with Joseph. His brothers' rejection of him was not accidental; it was necessary. It meant riches for the world, life to the dead.

In the crowning narrative of Genesis, Joseph continues to speak to his frightened and amazed brothers. He says,

> And now, do not be distressed and do not be angry with yourselves for selling me here, because it was to save lives that God sent me ahead of you. For two years now there has been famine in the land, and for the next five years there will not be plowing and reaping. But God sent me ahead of you to preserve for you a remnant on earth and to save your lives by a great deliverance. So then, it was not you who sent me here, but God.[5]

Just as Joseph was sent ahead of his brothers to preserve a remnant on earth and to save lives by a great deliverance, so too Messiah has been sent ahead of Israel to preserve a remnant and to save lives by a great deliverance.

We are not trifling with the text nor are we bending things to force the Hebrew Scriptures into the shape of Christian interpretations. If we let the story tell itself, the picture is simple and clear. Joseph is a redeemer of Israel. He is a demonstration of how God does redemption. He is a portrait of what the LORD's redeeming agent looks like.

The shadow cast by Joseph's character is so clearly Messianic that the sages of the Talmud adopted the title "Messiah son of Joseph" to describe the suffering servant Messiah prophesied in Isaiah and Zechariah. In those interpretations, the Messianic office was split into two. The suffering and afflicted Messiah was named Messiah ben Joseph, perhaps because His redemptive sufferings were reminiscent of the difficulties through which Joseph suffered. The victorious, conquering Messiah was called Messiah ben David because He was the Davidic descendent coming to rule over Israel.

For example, tractate *Sukkot*[6] suggests the passage in Zechariah 12 which says, "They will look on me, the one they have pierced, and they will mourn for him as one mourns for an only child," is a reference to the death of Messiah ben Joseph, who dies while redeeming Israel. In the two-Messiah interpretations, the Joseph-Messiah was destined to die in the redemption process.

In the Gospels, Philip the disciple introduces the Master to Nathaniel as Yeshua ben Yoseif, Jesus the son of Joseph, the one that Moses wrote about in the Torah, the one the prophets wrote about.

Who is Benjamin?

The temptation to push the analogy is too great, and I have succumbed. In our Messianic interpretation of the Joseph story, the Joseph character symbolizes Messiah, and Joseph's eleven brothers symbolize Israel. But among the brothers is the odd character of Benjamin. Benjamin is the silent, yet key player in the whole narrative.

Who is Benjamin? He is the younger son of Rachel. He was not part of the rejection of Joseph. He was not party to the deception of Jacob. Where does Benjamin fit into the picture we are painting? What is his role among the brothers?

If we apply to Benjamin the same *midrashic* reading which we have applied to the story of Joseph—if we apply this same methodology to Benjamin—who is he? What is Benjamin's role in the Messianic interpretive?

Once the question is posed, the answer follows quickly. Benjamin is the brother who did not reject Joseph. He is the brother who did not sell Joseph to the Egyptians. At the time the unpleasant incident happened, he was just a child. In fact, Benjamin seems to vanish from the narrative and to be all but forgotten until he reemerges here at the end of the story.

Perhaps this is too much for our critical sensibilities. Perhaps I have pushed the symbolic interpretation of the literal text too far now. But if I have, be patient and at least enjoy the metaphor with me.

Who is Benjamin? If the other ten brothers represent Israel's rejection of Messiah, Benjamin must represent that portion of Israel that did not reject Messiah. In the narrative, Benjamin has a place among the brothers. He is one of the sons of Israel, but he never abandoned Joseph. By way of analogy, he can only be believing-Judaism. Benjamin must represent the believing remnant of Israel that did not reject Messiah.

In the days of the Master, Benjamin was the disciples, the *talmidim*, the believers, the *Notzrim*, the Nazarene sect, those called *HaDerek*, The Way. Benjamin was believing-Israel. Benjamin! The Jewish believers.

In our Genesis narrative, it is with Benjamin that Joseph has hidden his cup. It is Benjamin who receives five times the portion from Joseph's table. He has the cup of the Master! He eats from the table of the Master! It is given unto Benjamin.

To put it into familiar terminology, Benjamin symbolizes authentic Messianic Judaism. The Apostle Paul was a product of first century Messianic Judaism. His amazing salvation story is a sort of paradigm for the Jewish experience with Messiah. His story involved a personal encounter with the Risen Master. In a vivid dramatization of the revelation of Yeshua to him, Paul was literally blinded and then his eyes were literally opened. His shock at the revelation of Messiah's identity was no less than any of the brothers' in Genesis 45.

By coincidence, Paul is the only Apostle to give us his tribal identity. In both Romans and Philippians Paul tells us that he is of the tribe of Benjamin. He is the paradigmatic Jewish believer, and by coincidence, he is a son of the tribe of Benjamin.

In the literal reading of biblical history, Benjamin is a small tribe of great consequence. At one point, the men of Benjamin became so immoral that all the other tribes turned against them. Out of Benjamin came the first King of Israel. Benjamin's geographically valuable territory contained the sacred city of Jerusalem. Benjamin was a buffer zone between the two powerful tribes of Ephraim and Judah. Ultimately Benjamin's territory was the strategic prize that the tribes battled for.

The Psalmist recognizes Benjamin's unique position. Psalm 68 creates a vision of a future day when God returns to His Temple in Jerusalem in great pomp and pageantry. Surprisingly, the little tribe of Benjamin leads the procession to the Temple.

> *Your procession has come into view, O God,*
> *The procession of my God and King into the sanctuary.*
> *In front are the singers, after them the musicians;*
> *With them are the maidens playing tambourines.*
> *Praise God in the great congregation;*
> *Praise the LORD in the assembly of Israel.*
> *There is the little tribe of Benjamin, leading them,*
> *There the great throng of Judah's princes,*
> *And there the princes of Zebulun and of Naphtali.*
> *Summon your power, O God;*
> *Show us your strength, O God,*
> *As you have done before.*
> *Because of your temple at Jerusalem kings will bring you gifts.*[7]

Jewish Believers

In the Joseph narratives, Benjamin is introduced at his birth and then disappears from the story until near the end. The same is true of believing-Judaism. She appeared on the scene in the Days of the Master, but quickly vanished from the record of history, only to reappear now as the story begins to culminate.

In the preceding century, we've seen the amazing fulfillment of many prophecies relating to the return of the Jewish people to the land of Israel. No less surprising than the formation of the modern state of Israel was the reappearance of believing-Judaism. To be sure, throughout Church history, there have always been Jewish converts. The Jewish believers within the Messianic Jewish movement (i.e. believing-Judaism), however, are something different. Messianic Jews claim that they are not Jewish converts to Christianity. Rather, they are Jewish believers retaining their full Jewish identity.

Modern Messianic Judaism is an odd hybrid of religious impetuses. The modern Messianic movement began as a missionary effort of the Evangelical Church. Who better to bring the Gospel to Jews than Jewish Christians? That was the reasoning. Jewish-Christian organizations began to reach out to the Jewish community in order to proselytize.

I can vividly remember my excitement as a young boy in small-town Minnesota when a Jewish speaker from Jews for Jesus came to our little Evangelical church to speak. I had never even met a real Jew before, much less a Messianic Jew! There were no Jews at all in our part of Minnesota. What's more, we were hosting him in our house for dinner.

I remember that my sister suggested we serve ham as a test of his conversion! She was joking, of course, but the theological assumption we made was that as a real Christian, he could have no qualms about eating pork.

We did not serve ham.

The idea of Jewish believers captured my heart and imagination. It was incredible. It was the most exciting thing to ever happen at my church. The idea! The possibility!

That was back in the early 1970's. Jews for Jesus was one example of the kind of Jewish outreach organizations that were actively using Jews as missionaries to pursue Jews for conversion.

As part of the attempt to reach Jews, these Jewish outreach missions began to imitate Judaism. The reasoning, as I see it, went something like this: "If we met on Saturday instead of Sunday, maybe Jews would feel more comfortable. If we did some synagogue liturgy instead of old hymns, maybe Jews would feel more comfortable. If we said 'Shalom' instead of 'Hello, How are you?' maybe Jews would feel more comfortable. If we say Yeshua instead of Jesus, if we say Rav Shaul instead of Paul, etc., maybe Jews would feel more comfortable." Surprisingly, one result of repackaging Christianity for Jewish consumption was a developing subculture within the Church that was uniquely Jewish.

The original intent of the missionaries was to spread Judaism like peanut butter on a piece of bread. The bread was traditional Christianity. But now it had a Jewish flavor. At best, it was a trick. A fake. The old bait and switch. It is unpleasant to admit, but the movement began as something of a façade conceived with the intent of luring Jews into the faith. In some ways, much of the façade still remains. From its very inception, such an enterprise flirts with disingenuousness and invites pretense and pretending. In terms of converts, the results have been under-whelming.

However, as a result of these missionary efforts, something unique began to happen. Not what was expected. The expected result was that Jews would pour into the Christian faith. That's not what happened. What did happen was something completely unintended. In the attempt to create an artificial Judaism, the Jewish missionary movement had hit upon something authentic: Torah.

When Messianic Judaism decided to meet on Shabbat so Jews would feel more comfortable, someone must have raised the obvious question, "Hey, isn't this the real biblical Shabbat anyway?" And when Messianic Judaism started doing the festivals to make Jews interested, someone must have pointed out that, "These festivals teach about Messiah. This stuff is all about Messiah!"

It was an amazing thing! Messianic Judaism had accidentally stumbled into Torah! The rediscovery of Torah continues to this day and promises to be the most enduring contribution to the faith that the whole Hebrew Roots movement will make.

What began as a ruse has begun to emerge as a reality. Believing-Judaism has begun to spawn small communities of Torah. Today, believing Jews are meeting in their own synagogues and congregations all over the world, living out Torah lives and retaining Jewish identity.

It is amazing because the world has not seen congregations of Jewish believers living Torah lives in obedience to the Master for almost 2000 years. Like Benjamin re-entering the Joseph story at the end of the narrative, believing-Judaism has returned.

If the effectiveness of the Messianic / Hebrew Roots movement was to be weighed in terms of how many Jews have been evangelized, we would have to say that, so far, it has been less than a fabulous success. But if we weigh the effectiveness of the movement in terms of how it has begun to restore Torah to the Body of Messiah at large, the results are impressive. When we see how it has begun to draw disenfranchised Jews back to their own heritage, back to Torah and to Messiah, and how it has begun to reveal to us the authentic, first century pattern of our faith, then we must admit that it has been a wild success. And it has just begun. Benjamin is awakening, and he is poised to reshape and restore the Faith to her biblical heritage.

In the Torah, Joseph will not reveal his identity to his brothers until Benjamin is brought before him. Thus, we might well expect that authentic believing-Judaism yet has a great role to play in the revelation of the identity of Messiah. However, if she is to play this part, she must be true to her own identity. Messianic Judaism must not pretend to be Jewish, rather she must live out her Jewishness as an authentic component of her faith in the Jewish Messiah.

These are exciting times.

Messianic Gentiles?

Another surprising and unanticipated result of the Messianic Jewish movement is the Gentile Christian response to the Torah mode of life and worship. Anyone around the Messianic Jewish movement is quick to observe the disproportionate numbers of non-Jews crowding into the Messianic synagogues. Oftentimes, when visiting a Messianic Jewish synagogue, one detects a distinct lack of Jews!

Ironically, the Messianic Jewish movement is becoming a largely Gentile phenomenon. Oftentimes, those who look the most Jewish (dressed in Jewish garb and such), are not Jews at all.

This is one of the strange things that give the movement a surreal quality. If you went to a Russian Orthodox church, you would expect most of the people to be Russian, or at least of Eastern European descent. If you went to an Ethiopian Coptic church, you'd expect most of the people to be Ethiopian. You would likely find Coptic Christians that weren't Ethiopian, but you certainly wouldn't expect to meet a Norwegian from Wisconsin who was pretending to be an Ethiopian!

Gentiles have been joining themselves to the Messianic Jewish movement for years. A lot of us Gentile believers don't always understand why we feel compelled to worship and live in a Torah mode. We aren't exactly sure of why we are drawn to Jewish expression. We don't necessarily feel like we fit in within Messianic Judaism, but then we certainly don't fit within the mainstream Church any longer either.

A short exposure to the Hebrew Roots of our faith is enough to ruin us for going back to our original churches. But where is there room for us in a religion defined by an ethnicity we do not share?

On the other hand, it is not unusual for Jewish believers to become frustrated with the Gentiles filling the seats of their synagogues. Many Jewish believers within the Messianic movement joined a Messianic synagogue because they were unhappy being the "token Jew" within a Christian church. Now they look around the synagogue and realize that they are again the "token Jews" in a congregation of non-Jews. At other times, Jewish believers have protested that the Gentile presence in their congregations serves as a deterrent to effective Jewish evangelism. Thus, it is often the case that the Gentiles, even though they may constitute a majority in some Messianic Jewish congregations, are less than welcome. There is often resentment and sometimes open hostility.

The end result for these bewildered Gentiles is a problem of identity. We aren't Jewish, but we often look like, worship like and live like Jews. So what are we? We are hard pressed to explain our passion for Torah.

This sense of identity crisis sends some of us searching back through our genealogical records trying to find a Jewish ancestor. We are searching our family trees, looking back through our old records for Jewish sounding names. "I must have a Jewish ancestor a few generations back. How else can I justify attending a Messianic synagogue?"

But even if I can prove that I have a Jewish ancestor does that somehow validate me? If I have a Jewish great-grandfather, am I therefore Jewish? Not according to the *halachah*. According to the legal determination of Jewishness, that simply makes me a Gentile with a Jewish great-grandfather. It may be of sentimental value to me, but it does not make me Jewish.

We find ourselves looking for some kind of validation for our presence in the Messianic community. If we cannot find a valid reason to explain ourselves and our identity, we are left with the uncomfortable possibility that we are merely posers and Jewish wannabes.

Posers and Wannabes

So what are the Gentiles doing here? How did all of this happen? How did we all get involved in a movement based upon an ethnicity we don't share?

The Gentile presence within the Messianic movement is another unwitting result of Jewish evangelism's accidental rediscovery of Torah. In the attempt to create an artificial Judaism, Messianic Judaism rediscovered an authenticity deeper and older than any form or structure existing within the mainstream Church: Torah. Suddenly, it wasn't primarily Jews coming into the movement. Rather, it was Christians, Gentile Christians who have been starved for authenticity for centuries. Gentile Christians hungry and zealous for Torah.

It was an accident. But when Messianic Judaism began to return to Torah in order to create a more Jewish venue, it struck a chord deep within the hearts of Christians everywhere. Suddenly Gentile Christians everywhere are responding, "Yes! This is what my faith has been missing. This is what I have always been looking for."

Gentile Christians within Messianic Judaism do not want to be regarded as posers or wannabes. But most of us would rather accept that denigration than let go of what we have discovered.

Not everyone in the Hebrew Roots movement is willing to be a poser though. On the other side is the Christian who is too authentic to pretend to be something he or she is not. I once heard a Christian teacher speaking for an hour about the Sabbath and all the wealth of riches that the Torah life offers to Judaism. He was clearly enthralled with the Jewish mode and clearly regarded it as the truly biblical walk of faith, but he concluded his lecture sadly. He said, "We Christians will always be on the outside, looking in."

There are vast numbers of Christians whose hearts long for the things of Torah, but feel that they cannot possess them, because those things are only for Jews. We are on the outside, looking in at Torah and Judaism like children pressing our noses to the window of a toy store. Our eyes are wide with excitement, but our hearts are heavy with the knowledge that we can never possess the things we see.

For Christians in this camp it is acceptable to read about and study about Judaism and Torah, but it is not acceptable to cross the line and begin to practice those things. To do so, we fear, would be legalism and Judaizing. Instead, we must go on with our regular church traditions. Of course, we would love to do Sabbath, our hearts leap at the thought, but the Sabbath is for Jews and we are Gentiles. Of course, we'd love to live a Torah life, but we are Gentile Christians, and Gentile Christians aren't under the Torah. So we must stay on our side of the glass. It's alright to look, but don't touch.

Those seem to be the only two options for Gentiles. We must either pretend and fake it or stay on the outside and look in longingly. But could there be a third way? A third option? There must be some middle ground, some kind of balance.

ENDNOTES

1 The relationship between Joseph and Yeshua is highlighted from extra-biblical Jewish traditions. The *Midrash Rabbah* tells us that Joseph did not drink of the fruit of the vine from the time he was separated from his brothers until he was reunited with them (*Bereishit Rabbah* 93:7). It also informs us that they cast lots for Joseph's coat (*Bereishit Rabbah* 84:8). The Testament of Zebulun tells us that Joseph was in the cistern for three days and three nights (Testament of Zebulun 4:4).

2 Chofetz Chaim cited in ArtScroll's *Stone Edition Chumash*. Scherman (1994).

3 Genesis 45:4,5

4 Romans 11:12

5 Genesis 45:6–8

6 Sukkot 52a

7 Psalm 68:24–29

The Sons of Joseph

5
The Sons of Joseph
Genesis 48

The old patriarch is dying. It won't be long. Joseph and his two sons have come to bid him farewell. The rest of Joseph's brothers have come too. They are all old men now with gray hair and beards themselves. They are grandfathers and even great-grandfathers. They are all assembled outside of the tent, waiting to be called. They hope to receive their father's blessing as he departs from the world, even as he received the blessing from his father Isaac who in turn received it from his father Abraham.

Joseph is called into the tent.

The many years of hardship and heartbreak have worn on Jacob. He looks frail and thin as he lifts himself from his bed. A servant admits Joseph into his presence.

Out of respect for his father, Joseph stands quietly, waiting for his father to break the silence. His wait is a short one. Jacob immediately begins to deliver the words he has been rehearsing in his mind. He says to Joseph, "God Almighty appeared to me at Luz in the land of Canaan, and there He blessed me and said to me, 'I am going to make you fruitful and will increase your numbers. I will make you a community of nations, and I will give this land as an everlasting possession to your seed after you.'"[1]

Joseph nods. This is not new information for him. This is a reiteration of the covenant promises given to his great-grandfather Abraham, then to his grandfather Isaac, and finally to his father Jacob. But why was his father telling him this? Did his father mean to pass this blessing on to him? Did his father intend to skip over his brothers, as Abraham had passed over Ishmael, as Isaac had passed over Esau? Was Joseph to be the sole inheritor of the promise of the seed?

However, Jacob has something else in mind. He continues speaking to his son saying, "Now then, your two sons born to you in Egypt before I came to you here will be reckoned as mine;

Ephraim and Manasseh will be mine, just as Reuben and Simeon are mine."[2]

It takes a moment for it to sink in, but when it does, Joseph smiles. He nods. He understands. His father Jacob intends to adopt his sons. By adopting Joseph's two sons, Ephraim and Manasseh, Jacob will elevate those two boys to a station of headship equal to the rest of Jacob's sons. Ephraim and Manasseh will become brothers of the twelve sons of Jacob. The two sons will double Joseph's standing among his brothers. When Jacob's inheritance is divided among his sons, Ephraim and Manasseh will each receive a portion equal with the other brothers. The result of the adoption maneuver will be to bestow a double portion of Jacob's inheritance upon the House of Joseph.

The double portion is the right of the firstborn. Even though Joseph is not actually the firstborn among the brothers, Jacob intends to insure that he be accorded the honor regardless.

Jacob's adoption of Joseph's two sons will also result in making Joseph's sons into his siblings! Thus, Joseph will become a "brother" of Ephraim and Manasseh.

Jacob goes on to explain his reason for bestowing this firstborn right upon Joseph. A shadow passes over his foggy eyes as he says, "While I was returning from Paddan, to my sorrow Rachel died in the land of Canaan while we were still on the way, a little distance from Ephrath. So I buried her there beside the road to Ephrath."[3] Joseph is Jacob's firstborn son through Rachel. Rachel was Jacob's first love and the only wife he ever intended to marry. In Jacob's mind, Joseph is the true firstborn. As a token of his affection for Rachel, he intends to accord the honor of firstborn to her son Joseph by adopting Ephraim and Manasseh as his own children.

Ephraim and Manasseh enter the tent of their grandfather. Their names mean Fruitfulness and Forgetfulness respectively. They are young men already. As they stand before the old patriarch and their father Joseph, they fidget nervously and shift their weight from foot to foot. They look more like Egyptians than they look like Hebrews. Their mother is the daughter of an Egyptian priest. They are dressed in the garments of the Egyptian court. Their hair is shaved in the Egyptian style. It is hardly any wonder that Jacob, with his failing eyes, says, "Who are these?"

It is an uncomfortable moment for Ephraim and Manasseh. Their grandfather does not recognize them. For a moment, they must feel that they surely do not belong in this tent or among this strange family of their father. But Joseph answers saying, "They are the sons God has given me here." With a genuine note of delight in his voice Jacob says, "Bring them to me so I may bless them."

Jacob wraps his frail old arms around Ephraim and kisses him. He embraces Manasseh and kisses him. The boys are visibly relieved to receive such a warm welcome from their grandfather. "I never expected to see your face again, and now God has allowed me to see your children too," Jacob says.[4]

Then, in keeping with the ancient ritual of adoption, Jacob sits the boys down on his lap. It is an awkward and comical shuffling about as the big teenagers find themselves being seated on the knees of this fragile old man. But this is the ancient ritual by which adoptions are made official, and rituals are sometimes awkward. As Joseph helps remove his sons from Jacob's knees, he realizes that they are no longer his sons. Instead, they are his brothers. In a gesture of gratitude, he bows down before Jacob with his face to the ground.

Now that Ephraim and Manasseh are his own sons, Jacob intends to give them the blessing of sons. He reaches out his hands to place them on the heads of the boys. But as he does so, he crosses his arms and places his right hand on Ephraim's head, though he is the younger, and he places his left hand on Manasseh's head, even though Manasseh is the firstborn.

Jacob takes a deep, rasping breath and draws the Spirit of prophecy into his lungs. Then he begins to bless the House of Joseph saying, "May the God before whom my fathers Abraham and Isaac walked, the God who has been my shepherd all my life to this day, the Angel who has delivered me from all harm—may He bless these boys. May they be called by my name and the names of my fathers Abraham and Isaac, and may they increase greatly upon the earth."[5]

When Joseph realizes that his father has placed his right hand on the head of Ephraim, the second born, he says, "No, my father, this one is the firstborn; put your right hand on his head." Joseph takes hold of Jacob's right hand to try to gently move it from Ephraim's head to Manasseh's head.

However, Jacob's inversion of the birth order is not accidental. He refuses and says, "I know, my son, I know. Manasseh too will become a people, and he too will become great. Nevertheless, his younger brother will be greater than he, and his seed will become a fullness of nations."[6]

Jacob knows that they will indeed be blessed. So abundant will be the blessing he has placed upon them that their names will become synonymous with blessing. He laughs out loud and says to his new sons, "In your name will Israel pronounce this blessing: 'May God make you like Ephraim and Manasseh.'"[7]

Fathers still bless their sons with these words even to this very day. Every Shabbat the father of the home lays his hands upon his sons and pronounces this blessing over them, "May God make you like Ephraim and Manasseh."

But what does it mean to be like Ephraim and Manasseh?

Like Ephraim and Manasseh

The Torah tells us that during Joseph's time of estrangement from his family, he took Asenath, an Egyptian bride. Through her, Joseph bore two sons, Ephraim and Manasseh. The two sons of Joseph and Asenath later went on to become patriarchs of two of the Twelve Tribes of Israel.

Unpleasant as it may be for the sages to admit, this is the plain meaning of the text. Ephraim and Manasseh are the sons of an Egyptian mother. Furthermore, they are raised in the Egyptian court. Aside from a common faith in the God of their father Joseph, they seem to have no identity among the sons of Israel. They are grandsons, but not sons. By all appearances, Ephraim and Manasseh are Gentiles, raised in a Gentile environment.

It was not until Jacob deliberately adopted Ephraim and Manasseh as sons that they received their identity as Sons of Israel, whereby they could take a direct share of the inheritance. When Jacob took the boys upon his knees in the rite of adoption, it accomplished more than giving a double portion of the inheritance to the House of Joseph. Subsequent to the adoption maneuver, Ephraim and Manasseh were accorded full status as sons of Israel. Their previous identities became irrelevant. Henceforth they were full-blooded sons of Israel regardless of their actual genealogical descent. They were no longer sons of Joseph and Asenath. They were sons of Israel.

Ephraim and Manasseh are not considered stepsons of Jacob, nor are they regarded as grandsons of Jacob. Rather, they are considered full-blooded sons. The Torah, of course, is not concerned with their Egyptian half-breed status because paternity determines identity. But subsequent to the adoption, neither their previous maternity nor paternity has any further bearing on their status. They are now full sons of Jacob. That is the result of the absolute power accorded to biblical adoptions.

We see an example of the absolute nature of the adoption ritual in the story of Samuel the prophet. Shmuel HaNavi was the firstborn son of an Ephraimite.[8] Yet, when his mother fulfilled her vow not to redeem Samuel, he was adopted by Eli the priest. Eli and his sons were the physical descendents of the Aaronic priesthood. According to Torah law, only an Aaronic priest descended from Aaron could ever serve in the priesthood. A Levite from any other family than that of Aaron was barred from serving as a priest. How much more so an Ephraimite! Yet, after the death of Eli, Samuel became the acting priest of Israel and was fully engaged in the priestly services, even conducting sacrifices on behalf of the entire nation. Samuel became a priest. But according to Torah law, Samuel the Ephraimite should not have been allowed to conduct sacrifices or serve in a priestly role. How do we understand this seeming contradiction?

Samuel was adopted by Eli. His previous tribal affiliations (whether Levite or Ephraimite or both) had no relevance subsequent to his adoption into the house of Eli. As an adopted son of Eli, Samuel became a descendent of Aaron and therefore qualified for the priestly service.

By rabbinic standards and *halachah,* adoption alone would not be sufficient grounds for Samuel's participation in the priesthood, but by biblical standards, adoption is absolute. Samuel's adoption into the house of Aaron is sufficient. All previous familial associations are no longer relevant. Biblical adoption is absolute.

By the same token, our measurement of Yeshua as a son of David relies on biblical adoption. Tribal affiliation was never determined through the mother because whatever tribe a woman married into became her new and absolute tribal identity. The Gospels do not purport to record Miriam's genealogy. Because, as a woman, her genealogy is not relevant after her betrothal and marriage to Joseph. Yeshua is regarded as a son of David not because of Miriam's bloodline, but because of Joseph's bloodline.[9]

But how is this possible when Yeshua's conception was without human agency? He is not, after all, the actual son of Joseph. Instead, Joseph adopts Him as his son when he marries Miriam. How is it that the Gospels can lay claim to Davidic descent for Yeshua, based upon Joseph's lineage, when they also deny that Joseph sired Yeshua? How can Yeshua be regarded as a Son of David? It works only because biblical adoption is absolute.

When Joseph married Miriam (and thereby adopted the as yet unborn Yeshua), Yeshua became Joseph's son in every right and respect. He was not the stepson or adopted son, he was Joseph's son, and thus an heir to Joseph's genealogy: the House of David.

Thus, we see through the examples of the adoptions of Samuel and Yeshua that biblical adoption is absolute. It erases any previous ethnic, tribal or family lines. So it is that when Ephraim and Manasseh were adopted by their grandfather Jacob, they became full sons of Israel.

Who Are Ephraim and Manasseh?

In the previous chapter, we applied a Messianic interpretation to the story of Joseph to determine a deeper meaning of the text. Joseph was sent to his brothers, sent to them by their father, by his own beloved father. He was rejected by them, stripped, put in the earth, and ultimately given over to the Gentiles. However, the rejection turned out to be in accordance with God's purpose and plan for Joseph—so he could rise to a position of sovereignty, from which he could extend salvation to all peoples, even to his own brothers. Adding to the richness of the analogy, Joseph's own brothers failed to recognize him because he had been among the Gentiles so long that he seemed to them to be a Gentile prince, and not a son of Israel. Only when he chose to reveal himself as Joseph did they realize his true identity.

The parallels between the story of Joseph and the story of Yeshua are too many, too precise and too great for people of faith to discard as coincidence. For this reason we identify the Joseph character as a type foreshadowing Yeshua. The story of Joseph runs parallel to the story of Yeshua.

Following the same line of inquiry, we asked if the character of Benjamin might also possess a typological significance. Benjamin was the brother who did not reject Joseph. He was the brother who did not sell Joseph to the Egyptians. He is all but forgotten in the text from his birth until he re-emerges near the end of the story. Indeed, it could be construed that Benjamin foreshadows believing-Judaism, the remnant of Jews who did not reject Messiah, but embraced Him.

Having come this far down a perilous (yet rewarding) road of Messianic interpretations, dare we go any further? If we apply the same methodologies and symbolic interpretations to Joseph's sons Ephraim and Manasseh, where do they stand in the story of Messiah? Who are Ephraim and Manasseh?

Jacob himself poses the same question when he first sees the two sons enter his tent. He says, "Who are these?"[10] The Torah means for us to ask the same question. Who are they? What is their significance in our reading of the story? Manasseh and Ephraim are the sons born to Joseph in those years while he was estranged from his brothers. They are Manasseh and Ephraim, "Forgetfulness" and "Fruitfulness." They are children raised in Gentile Egypt, sons of Joseph's Gentile bride.

Who are they in the *midrash* we are spinning? They are Gentile Christians: non-Jewish believers. They are the followers of Jesus. They are those born in the years while Messiah is estranged from His brothers. They are called "Forgetfulness" and "Fruitfulness." We Gentiles may have forgotten the house of Jacob, but we have been fruitful. We are like the children raised in Egypt, sons of an Egyptian bride, thoroughly Egyptians!

During our long estrangement from the House of Jacob, we have maintained a faith in the God of Abraham, Isaac and Jacob. Our faith was transmitted to us through Yeshua, just as Ephraim and Manasseh maintained faith in the God of Abraham only through the testimony of their father Joseph. Like Ephraim and Manasseh, we have been complete strangers to Jacob and the sons of Israel.

But now, through the firstborn rights conferred upon Messiah, the only begotten of the Father, an amazing reversal of fortune has befallen us. Jacob took Ephraim and Manasseh on his knees in the rite of adoption. So too, we have been adopted into Israel. Like Ephraim and Manasseh we are no longer to be regarded as foreigners to Israel but as fellow citizens.[11] Like Ephraim and Manasseh, we are adopted sons.[12] Like Ephraim and Manasseh, we have received full rights as sons.[13] Like Ephraim and Manasseh, we have become heirs together with Israel.[14] Like Ephraim and Manasseh, we have been grafted into the family tree of Israel.[15] Just as Ephraim and Manasseh were raised to the level of brethren with Joseph, so too we have been raised to the level of brothers with Messiah.[16]

Isn't this the story the Torah is telling us here? We have been brought into Israel, adopted into Israel, as part of the firstborn rights of Yeshua. We have a share in His inheritance, and we have been raised to the level of His brethren. This is our spiritual inheritance!

However, it is a radically different theology than the Church has historically taught. Historically we have taught a theology of replacement and substitution by which we believe the Church has replaced and even superceded Israel. We have believed that the Church is the New Israel. We have taught that if Jews want any inheritance in the covenants, they must forsake Judaism and convert to Christianity. This is not the Torah picture.

According to the story of Ephraim and Manasseh, it is not Israel that will be joined to the Church; it is the Church that has been joined to Israel! Gentile Christians are adopted into Israel with full rights of sonship. It is Israel we are adopted into, not vice-versa. Moreover, because the biblical adoption is absolute, we are guaranteed full standing in Israel. We are not second-class citizens. We are not stepsons or even grandsons. We are as much a genuine part of the family as a full-blooded Jew. After all, Paul tells us, even the natural born Israelite is an adopted child, adopted by God.[17]

This does not mean that Gentile believers are Jewish. But it does mean that we have as much a place in Israel as a Jew. It means that we have a right to the Sabbath. It is part of our inheritance in Israel. We have a right to the festivals. They are part of our inheritance in Israel. We have a right to the Torah. It is part of our inheritance in Israel. We have a right to say "Abraham our Father,"

"Isaac our Father," "Jacob our Father" because we have been joined to the family of Israel. It is part of our inheritance in Israel.

The good news for Gentiles within the Torah movement is that we no longer should feel compelled to find that elusive Jew in the genealogy. We don't need to find some external validation for our participation in the community of Torah. The inheritance is already ours. We don't need to pose. We don't need to feel like pretenders. We have full participation.

To be a genuine part of Israel, we don't need to tell Yiddish jokes, eat gefilte fish or wear a yarmulke. (Although I recommend the fish. It's not too bad.) Our position is guaranteed in Messiah. It is our place to grab hold of the fringes of His garment. It is our place, our inheritance, our standing among the tribes of Israel.

The Seed of Ephraim

But is it at all likely that Paul, in the process of his research, made any of these spurious connections? He was certainly familiar with rabbinic methodologies and *midrashic* retellings. For example, his treatment of Sarah and Hagar in Galatians 4 is merely a reworking of an old rabbinic *midrash* on Sarah and Isaac. Paul was not above allegorical reinterpretation. But it hardly seems likely that Paul, during his reading of the stories, would have crawled out on an allegorical limb as far as we have, were it not for one small detail. As Jacob blessed his newly adopted sons, Ephraim and Manasseh, he declared over Ephraim, "His seed will become a fullness of nations."[18]

We have already seen how Paul interpreted the seed promises of Abraham to refer specifically to Messiah, the singular seed of Abraham. Paul went on to posit, "If you belong to Messiah, then you are Abraham's seed." The Gentile believers have been adopted through Messiah, engrafted into Israel through Messiah. The Gentile converts, immersed in Messiah, have been recreated as the seed of Abraham.[19] To Paul, the words, "All nations will be blessed in your seed," constituted the mystery of the Gospel and the basis for the Gentile inclusion. Seeing how those seed promises were so fundamental to Pauline theology, it would be surprising if he had not paused to consider the implication of Jacob's words, "His seed will become a fullness of nations."

Recall that in Romans chapter 11 Paul compared Israel to an olive tree by way of analogy. He explained to his Gentile readers in Rome that they had been adopted into the family tree of Israel. They were adopted like wild olive branches taken from other olive trees (other nations) and grafted into the olive tree of Israel. The result of the engrafting was that they had become a full part of the olive tree of Israel. They were no longer Gentiles in the strict sense, but instead had become heirs with Israel.

But remember how Paul warned the Gentiles not to become arrogant over the natural branches. Rather, they should remember that as engrafted branches, they are the guests. He admitted that some of the natural branches (Jews) had been removed from the tree because of their unbelief. But even this unbelief he explains away as a necessary and temporary state to allow time for the nations to come to faith.

In Romans 11:25 he summarized this thought by saying, "I do not want you to be ignorant of this mystery, brothers, so that you may not be conceited: Israel has experienced a hardening in part until the fullness of the Gentiles has come in."

"Fullness of the Gentiles" is the phrase that Jacob used to bless his newly adopted son Ephraim. Jacob said to Ephraim, "Your seed will be a fullness of the Gentiles (nations)."[20]

By invoking Ephraim's "fullness of the Gentiles," Paul perhaps means to infer that the Gentile believers adopted into Israel are to be regarded as the seed of Ephraim, a fullness of the Gentiles (nations) and the ultimate extension of the Abrahamic seed promises.

Like Ephraim the son of Joseph, who was himself adopted by Israel, the Gentile believers are Messiah ben Joseph's Gentile progeny, adopted into Israel.[21] The Gentile believers are part of the Fullness of Nations.

ENDNOTES

1 Genesis 48:3,4 translating *kehilat amim* as "community of nations."

2 Genesis 48:5

3 Genesis 48:7,8

4 Genesis 48:8–11

5 Genesis 48:15–16

6 Genesis 48:19

7 Genesis 48:20

8 But of Levitical stock according to 1 Chronicles 6.

9 The prevailing opinion, however, is that the genealogy recorded in the book of Luke is through Miriam, not Yosef. The Gospel reader will note that the text itself makes no such indication.

10 Genesis 48:8

11 Ephesians 2:19

12 Ephesians 1:5

13 Galatians 4:5

14 Ephesians 3:6

15 Romans 11

16 Hebrews 2:11–17

17 Romans 9:4

18 Genesis 48:19

19 Galatians 3:26–29

20 A textual comparison of Romans 11:25 and Genesis 48:19 raises the possibility that Paul was directly alluding to this passage of Torah. However, if he was, he did not use the Lxx wording of the passage which translates it as "a multitude of nations." Paul's wording is a more literal rendering of the Hebrew.

21 It is not meant to be taken in a literal sense, because the promise of all nations being blessed in the seed is already literally fulfilled in Messiah. The Ephraim allusion of Romans 11:25 is not a reference to the physical descendents of Abraham or Ephraim, but rather to those who belong to Messiah.

The Exodus

6
The Exodus
Exodus 14

"In every generation it is one's duty to regard himself as though he personally had gone out of Egypt, as it is written: 'You shall tell your son on that day: "It was because of this that the LORD did for me when I went out of Egypt."' It was not only our fathers whom the Holy One redeemed from slavery; we, too, were redeemed with them." (*Passover Haggadah* quoting Exodus 13:8).

On the Eve of Passover, at every Passover Seder meal, those words are recited from the Passover Haggadah. In a similar way, the Master Himself commands all of His disciples (in every generation) to do Passover in remembrance of Him. Passover and the Feast of Unleavened Bread are what He referred to when He said, "Do this in remembrance of me."

But can a Gentile legitimately participate in the Passover?[1] It is a question that must have occurred to Paul as he worked out the details of the mystery of the Gospel. He wrote to the Corinthian congregation, "For Messiah, our Passover lamb, has been sacrificed. Therefore let us keep the Festival..."[2]

Yet how could a Gentile keep Passover? Was it not an exclusively Jewish celebration?

For at least the duration of this chapter, let's fulfill the Haggadah's mandate and imagine ourselves as if we personally had gone out of Egypt. Whether you are Jewish or not, imagine that you and I are part of the Exodus. We, personally, have gone out of Egypt.

From our earliest memories, we recall the stories. They are the stories our father told us, late at night, after the sun had set, and our eyes were growing heavy as we were falling asleep. He told us about how we are all the sons and daughters of one father, a man named Abraham. He told us how it had come to pass that in days long, long ago, Abraham our father had made a covenant with a god, ADONAI, the LORD. Our father told us how this strange

God had made promises to Abraham, and what strange promises they were! "All nations will be blessed... your seed will inherit this land." A distant land. A promised land. And our father told us how this God had said to Abraham, "Know for certain that your descendants will be enslaved and oppressed four hundred years. But I will judge the nation whom they will serve, and afterward they will come out with many possessions."[3]

There were more stories. He told us the stories of Isaac and the stories of Jacob. He told us of Joseph and how we first came to be in Egypt. We learned of Joseph's wife, an Egyptian princess! Imagine it. Us—the sons and daughters of royalty! And by the dim lamplight of the deep Egyptian nights he whispered to us the last words of Joseph, "God will surely take care of you and bring you up from this land to the land which He promised on oath to Abraham, to Isaac and to Jacob."[4] These are our stories. This is our heritage.

Yet, there were other stories. There were stories of how the previous Pharaoh sought to destroy us. Casting the babies into the Nile. The hard oppression. The bitterness of slavery. The infants cemented alive into the brickwork of Egypt. The stories of our fathers and the God of our fathers seemed very much removed from the reality of our daily lives.

So, when Moses came to us with a message from the LORD, the God of Abraham, we were skeptical. When Moses said, this is what the LORD says, "I will bring you out from under the burdens of the Egyptians, and I will deliver you from their bondage. I will also redeem you with an outstretched arm and with great judgments. Then I will take you for my people, and I will be your God; and you shall know that I am the LORD your God, who brought you out from under the burdens of the Egyptians,"[5] we were more than a little skeptical.

We had heard of the LORD. We had cried out to Him; we had called to Him; we had longed for Him, we had even worshipped Him from afar—a God we had never seen. He was a God of long ago, a distant and remote God. The God of Abraham. But there were other gods in Egypt too; gods that we could see, gods that we could touch. The Egyptian gods were everywhere, all around us. They required no great leap of faith. We had built their temples with our own hands. And then, of course, there is Pharaoh, allegedly a god, a man, a god on earth, an immortal, clothed in mortal flesh.

Contest of the Gods

Despite what Moses might have heard, the fact is that we belong to Pharaoh; we are Pharaoh's people. Moses tells us we will be the People of God, but we are not God's people and He, in day-to-day reality, is not our God. We are Pharaoh's people, and like it or not, Pharaoh has exalted himself over us; he is our god. The gods of Egypt are our gods because they dominate us. It is not a matter of choice on our part. It is not a matter of faith or conviction; it is the simple, ugly fact. We belong to Egypt; we belong to Pharaoh; we belong to the gods of Egypt. We are property. We are owned.

So, if what Moses is saying turns out to be actually true, it will be a problem! It means that there will have to be a showdown, a contest of the gods.

As participants in the Exodus from Egypt, we were witnesses to that contest. We saw the great war between the gods unfold. The battle lines were drawn up like a chess game. On the one side was the LORD, "God of the Hebrews," and on the other was the mighty Egyptian pantheon. The Egyptian gods were represented on the playing board by a human incarnation in the person of Pharaoh: Pharaoh the supposed man-god, fully human, fully god. He was an Egyptian deity in the flesh. In order to challenge him, the LORD also needed a human representative, a sort of incarnation, a sort of god-man to carry out the contest. Moses was chosen to fill the role as it is written, "Then the LORD said to Moses, 'See, I make you as God to Pharaoh, and your brother Aaron shall be your prophet.'"[6]

And that's how we saw it. In the drama that unfolded before our eyes, Moses played the role of the LORD, opposite Pharaoh, who played the role of Egyptian god. Aaron played the role of the prophet of God, manifesting the power of the LORD opposite the magicians of Egypt, who manifested the powers of the Egyptian deities. Those were the pieces on the playing board in the contest of the gods.

At the first, Pharaoh had never even heard of the LORD. He said to Moses and Aaron, "Who is the LORD that I should obey His voice to let Israel go? I do not know the LORD, and besides,

I will not let Israel go."[7] To Pharaoh, the god-king of the world's mightiest nation, Moses and Aaron must have presented a great insult. How dare some obscure Hebrew deity make a claim on his people? His slaves! Imagine the audacity of Moses and Aaron to suggest that Pharaoh, god-king of Egypt, respect the wishes of the deity of his slaves. Pharaoh replied, "Who is the LORD that I, Pharaoh, should obey him? I've never even heard of him!"

But it was not Pharaoh alone who needed convincing. We Hebrews were ready and willing to admit to the existence of the LORD, but the question for us was, "Will this old fairy-tale God of our fathers really be able to stand up to the gods of superpower Egypt, the most powerful nation in the world?" Indeed, He was able to stand, and in fear and trembling, we saw His glory revealed. Through the course of the ten plagues, we saw Him strike down the gods of Egypt.

The Egyptian pantheon was supposed to be in control of the forces of nature. There was a god of the Nile, but the Nile turned to blood. The goddess of fruitfulness, symbolized by the frog totem, was mocked with a plague of frogs. The sun god, chief of the Egyptian pantheon, was blotted out in the plague of darkness. Then, in the final plague, the slaying of the firstborn, the man-god Pharaoh himself was shown to be powerless as his firstborn son (also a man-god) was found dead.

Remember Passover? The terrible urgency. The slaughtering knife. The lamb. We dipped the hyssop, smeared the blood, our children stood watching.

Through the night, we waited. Our belongings were packed. We ate a hasty meal: lamb, unleavened bread, bitter herbs. We were waiting for death. We were waiting for deliverance.

The night wore on while the full moon passed over the waters and monuments of Egypt. We listened to the silence. Our cloaks were tucked into our belts. Our staffs were in hand. Suddenly a sound. A scream rising in the night. Another cry, another shout, wailing. Terror in the night, death wandering the streets of Egypt. Then the word came to us, and we left.

God's Reputation

As individuals in the middle of this unfolding drama, concerned only with our own little lives, our own personal redemption and our own personal salvation, we might not see the bigger picture of what is happening to us. We might not ever stop to ask ourselves, "Why should God Almighty care to redeem us from Egypt anyway? We've done nothing to merit His grace and favor. And why should He do it in this manner, causing pain and suffering to the Egyptians? Why the plagues? Why the gratuitous display of power?" Though we, as mere escaping slaves, might not have the wherewithal to ask these questions, God answers the questions anyway. It is a matter of reputation. His reputation.

The Exodus from Egypt was God's opportunity to "declare His Name." He used the redemption of Israel to establish His reputation. Consider the following Scriptures pulled from the Exodus narrative. Each one is offered by God as His rationalization behind the plagues on Egypt and the deliverance of Israel.

- The Egyptians will know I am the LORD (Exodus 7:5).
- That you may know there is no one like the LORD our God (Exodus 7:10).
- So that you will know that I, the LORD, am in this land (Exodus 8:22).
- In order to show you my power and in order to proclaim my Name through all the earth (Exodus 9:16).
- That you may tell your children and grandchildren… that you may know I am the LORD (Exodus 10:2).
- Against all the gods of Egypt I will execute judgments—I am the LORD (Exodus 12:12).
- I will be honored through Pharaoh and all his army, and the Egyptians will know that I am the LORD (Exodus 14:4).

Why did God do all this? Why the big display of power? Why the contest? Why is He redeeming Israel? In order to show His power and in order to proclaim His Name through all the earth.

For the LORD, the contest of the gods is a demonstration of His sovereignty. Through the events of the Exodus story, God is establishing His Name in the earth. He is making His entrance onto the stage of world history. In redeeming Israel, God is sending a clear message to the whole world, "I exist, I am God, there is none like Me!" He is sending a message to the false gods of the world. He is demonstrating that He alone is God, and there is none other.

We are His trophies. Our redemption from Egypt serves His purpose, which is the establishment of His Name. We are part of something much bigger than just getting out of making bricks; we are part of a plan to reveal God's eternal glory to "gods" and men. We are to be like trophies of victory in the banquet hall of the King.

However, none of these grand theological notions are likely to occur to us as we leave Egypt. Our only thought is our personal salvation. For the moment, it is hard to see the bigger picture.

The Camp by the Sea

Even with the slaying of the firstborn of Egypt and Pharaoh's consent to let us go, the contest of the gods has not yet been fully decided. Moses and Aaron had asked only that we be allowed to leave to celebrate a three-day festival to the LORD. We still belong to Pharaoh. He has given us leave to stretch our legs, and that's all.

We have arrived at the shore of the Red Sea. We are setting up tents, lighting cooking fires, and preparing to settle in for the night. Animals are braying, children are running about, dodging their mothers. Our young men are taking their first taste of freedom; the old ones are smiling to themselves. The day is beginning to fade, and we are tired after our journey. The waters of the sea are to the east; the wilderness of Egypt is to the west. Looming above our heads is the strange and awe-inspiring pillar of cloud.

We are a vast number of people, a mixed multitude.[8] Pharaoh wasn't partial to Hebrews. He took slaves from all nations. The camp of Israel now includes the tents of many nations. There were many peoples among the slave camps of Pharaoh; many who saw the light in the midst of the plague of darkness. There are many among us (I myself, for example) who saw how God had differentiated between the Egyptians and the Israelites. So, when we saw the Israelites marking their doorways with blood, we took refuge with them under the same blood. We are those who have left Egypt with Israel, and now we have set up our tents in the midst of their camp.

Pharaoh, however, makes no distinction between the Hebrews and the non-Hebrews. We are all slaves to him.

As the sun sets on Egypt, we look back toward the land from which we have come. As we look into the reddening western sky, we see what at first appears to be smoke. Is Egypt burning? Perhaps the LORD has poured out fire on it as he did to Sodom after Lot had left. But as we peer into the sunset, it seems that the smoke is coming closer. Perhaps it is not smoke. Perhaps it is a sandstorm, a mighty wind blowing out of Egypt.

Mothers are taking the children into their arms. Men stop driving tent stakes and lift their eyes to see this strange sight. A feeling of uneasiness begins to spread through the camp.

Then we hear a low rumbling. At first, it is like the sound of distant thunder. But unlike thunder, it is sustained and seems to come up from the ground. Slowly we realize, it is not smoke; it is not wind; it is the dust being kicked up from Pharaoh's horses and chariots. Even now, we can see the silhouettes of his horses and chariots coming out of the sunset.

"As Pharaoh drew near, the sons of Israel looked, and behold, the Egyptians were marching after them, and they became very frightened; so the sons of Israel cried out to the LORD."[9]

Panic spreads through the camp. There is no place to run to. There is no escape. Death pursues us; death is in front of us. Women are shrieking; men are cursing. A baby is crying. Miriam, the sister of Moses, lets her tambourine slip from her hand. By now, the sounds of hooves pounding the desert floor and the shouts of the charioteers are clear. Pharaoh—our god—is coming for us.

At this point, we cry out to Moses, "Is it because there were no graves in Egypt that you have taken us away to die in the wilderness?"[10] This Red Sea experience is about death and dying. In front of us is the sea. If we try to escape through it, we will drown and die. Behind us are the Egyptians. If we face the Egyptians, we will die.

Immersion and Conversion

As Paul wrote to the mixed multitude at Corinth, (a congregation of Jews and Gentiles who were proving to be no less a headache for him than the Exodus generation had been for Moses) he made a passing comment about this passage of Torah. He said, "For I do not want you to be unaware, brethren, that our fathers were all under the cloud and all passed through the sea; and all were immersed into Moses in the cloud and in the sea" (1 Corinthians 10:1).

Paul compares the crossing of the sea to immersion. Believers generally have different ideas about how baptism should be done, but what might surprise us all is that baptism was not originally a Christian ritual. It was a Jewish ritual. From the days of Moses, immersion (baptism) was regularly practiced by all of Israel. Anyone who became ritually unclean needed to undergo an immersion before they could enter the Temple. The priests immersed every day. After a woman completed menstruation, she needed to immerse herself before she could rejoin her husband. Those who had become contaminated in any way (i.e. lepers) needed to go through immersion before they were deemed ritually pure again. In Judaism, immersions like this are referred to as immersion into a "*mikvah.*" *Mikvah* is a Hebrew word meaning, "gathering of water." A *mikvah* could be a river, a lake, a spring, or any naturally fed gathering of water. Immersion in a *mikvah* was a regular part of Jewish life.

All worshippers going up to the Temple were required to first immerse themselves. Modern day visitors to Jerusalem can see the remains of the *mikvahoht* at the foot of the Temple steps. They are a regular feature of Jewish archaeological sites. There are immersion baths on Masada, at the Herodian, at Qumran and all over the land of Israel. It was forbidden to come into the presence of God within His Temple without first passing through a *mikvah.*

According to Judaism, a Gentile who wants to become Jewish must undergo several ritual requirements. For men, the two main requirements are circumcision and immersion. For a woman, immersion itself is the entire conversion ritual. In Jewish thought, a Gentile who converts to Judaism is still a Gentile until he comes up out of the water of the *mikvah.* Going down into the water, the convert is said to die to his old life. As he comes up, he is as a newborn child, a new creature.

Born Again

The term "born again" was not coined in the early 1970's when it began to appear on American bumper stickers, nor was it invented by Yeshua or the writers of the Apostolic scriptures. Rather, it was a rabbinic term for a Gentile who underwent a formal conversion to Judaism.

In the Talmud, this concept is expressed in tractate Yevamot: "When he comes up after his immersion, he is deemed an Israelite in all respects" (Yevamot 47b).

Rabbi Yose said, "One who has become a proselyte is like a child newly born" (Yevamot 48b).

In his book *The Waters of Eden*, Rabbi Aryeh Kaplan comments on the imagery of being born again through the *mikvah*:

> Emerging from the *mikvah* is very much like a process of rebirth. Seen in this light, we see that the *mikvah* represents the womb. When an individual enters the *mikvah*, he is reentering the womb, and when he emerges, he is as if born anew. Thus, he attains a completely new status... When a person immerses in the *mikvah*, he is placing himself in the state of the world yet unborn, subjecting himself totally to God's creative power.
>
> When a person immerses himself in water, he places himself in an environment where he cannot live. Were he to remain submerged for more than a few moments, he would die from lack of air. He is thus literally placing himself in a state of non-existence and non-life. Breath is the very essence of life, and, according to the Torah, a person who stops breathing is no longer considered among the living. Thus, when a person submerges himself in a *mikvah*, he momentarily enters the realm of the nonliving. When he emerges, he is like one reborn.
>
> To some degree, this explains why a *mikvah* cannot be made in a vessel or tub, but must be built directly in the ground, for in a sense, the *mikvah* also represents the grave. When a person immerses, he is temporarily in a state of death, and when he emerges, he is resurrected with a new status.

> We therefore see that immersion in the *mikvah* represents renewal and rebirth. [11]

"Like one reborn" is a general Talmudic way of speaking about proselytes. The rebirth of Gentiles who passed through the *mikvah* was taken literally by the sages. Gentiles born again as Jews were regarded as having no kin. In a legal sense, they were regarded as completely new creatures. Old family ties and relations were considered defunct, as if the convert had actually died and then come back to life as a different person.

Understanding that the term "born again" originally referred to a Gentile who had undergone conversion to Judaism clears up a difficult passage from the book of John. In John 3, Yeshua and the famous sage Nicodemus[12] are engaged in conversation about being "born again."

In our churches, we have always assumed that Yeshua coined the phrase "born again" in His conversation with Nicodemus. Nicodemus puzzled, "How can a man be born when he is old? He cannot enter a second time into his mother's womb and be born, can he?" (John 3:4). According to our traditional understanding of the passage, Nicodemus, a Sage on the Sanhedrin, was baffled by Yeshua's use of figurative language. Rather thickheaded, wouldn't you say?

However, in the Jewish context, the phrase "born again" was already in use. A born-again person was a Gentile who had converted to Judaism under the auspices of the rabbinic ritual. It referred to the symbolic death and rebirth the convert underwent as he passed through the waters of baptism. In Judaism, immersion is used as a conversion ritual. The *mikvah* is regarded as both a grave, in which the immersed dies, and a womb from which the immersed is reborn. "When an individual enters the *mikvah*, he is reentering the womb, and when he emerges, he is as if born anew," Rabbi Kaplan wrote.

In light of this context, we can better understand the conversation of John 3:3–10. When Nicodemus objects and says, "How can a man be born when he is old?" it is not because the figurative language has left him baffled. Rather, he is employing the same metaphorical terminology that Yeshua was using.

According to that imagery, Nicodemus was objecting by saying, "I am already Jewish. How can I convert to Judaism?"

Yeshua answers, "A man must be born of water and spirit." In other words, Yeshua tells Nicodemus that it is not enough to simply be Jewish. To be ethnically Jewish, or even to be a convert to Judaism via the rabbinic ritual, is not adequate for entrance to the Kingdom of Heaven. A spiritual conversion of the heart is the conversion experience that is really necessary. In essence, Yeshua is warning Nicodemus not to rely on his ethnicity (that is his Jewishness) for salvation. "You need to have a converted heart," Yeshua tells him.

Dead and Alive

Paul understood the death and rebirth imagery of the immersion ritual as well. He applied the ritual's imagery to those in Messiah in a very similar manner. Nowhere is this clearer than in Romans chapter 6 where he compares the conversion rite of a believer's immersion to the death and resurrection of Yeshua.

> Do you not know that all of us who have been immersed into Messiah Yeshua have been immersed into His death? Therefore, we have been buried with Him through immersion into death, so that as Messiah was raised from the dead through the glory of the Father, so we too might walk in newness of life. For if we have become united with Him in the likeness of His death, certainly we shall also be in the likeness of His resurrection. (Romans 6:3–5)

Paul is invoking the rubrics of the rabbinic conversion ceremony to teach us about the transformation that occurs when we place faith in Messiah. Just as in the rabbinic ritual, the Gentile is said to die to his old life and identity, Paul tells us that as we place faith in Messiah, we actually do die to our old lives and identities. Just as in the rabbinic ritual, the proselyte coming up out of the water of immersion is regarded as a new creature, so too we are to actually be regarded as new creatures, walking in newness of life. What is the newness of life? It is the resurrected Messiah within us.

Thanks to this mystical immersion into Messiah (not the actual ritual of immersion, but that spiritual transaction of faith and redemption) we are reborn with a completely new identity. We are no longer who we used to be. We are no longer the old person. That identity is legally dead.

The sages of the Talmud explained, "When the proselyte comes up after his immersion he is deemed to be an Israelite in all respects" (Yevamot 47b). Our immersion into Messiah transforms us as well, not a transformation of ethnicity, but a transformation of spirit. We are transformed into the image of Messiah. We are remade, reborn, renewed and recreated in the living water of Yeshua. As we emerge, our lives are totally different. They must be totally different.

Perhaps we don't always feel totally different. It is very likely that the average Greek didn't feel very Jewish as he stepped out of the water of immersion either. But legally, according to the rabbinic standard, he was. It might take that Greek a while to learn to live up to his new identity, but he was "regarded an Israelite in all respects" regardless of how he felt about it.

This isn't to say that Paul was endorsing the rabbinic ritual for proselytes. Far from it. We will see in later chapters that it was this very ritual Paul was arguing against. Rather, he has appropriated its symbolism (just as Yeshua did in John 3) and is applying it to all who have placed faith in Messiah.

The rabbinic conversion ritual is not biblical. By every standard except the rabbinic *halachah*, the Irishman who passes through the immersion of rabbinical conversion is nothing more than a wet Irishman.

The immersion into Messiah, however, is biblical. By God's standard, the Irishman who has immersed himself into faith in Messiah is no longer just an Irishman; he is the resurrected life of Yeshua, a whole new creature. His entire life is different. He has a new identity, a new nature, a new purpose and a new destiny. The old man is no more. He is remade and made alive. He is born again.

When writing to those in Corinth, Paul compared the crossing of the Red Sea to immersion. They were all under the cloud and all passed through the sea. They were all immersed into Moses in the cloud and in the sea.

Deeper into the Water

That night, by the light of the burning pillar, Moses lifts his hand over the sea. From across the water comes a cool breeze. A shiver through the spine. The breeze grows to a gentle wind, and still strengthens. Ripples form on the water, etching out the lines of a path across the surface. There is an excited murmuring among the people, and the wind increases. It is soon difficult to stand facing the wind. It feels as if the very breath of God is blasting across the water. Waves are crashing. Miriam picks up her tambourine. Suddenly, shooting across the water like the wake behind a sailing boat comes a line, a mark of division. With a roar like many waterfalls, the water splits to the left and to the right. It mounts and climbs, frothing and spraying, churning and splashing until it has formed a passage. It comes to rest, a wall of water on the left, and a wall of water on the right.

Now see in your mind the thousands and thousands of the host of Israel descending into the sea, to walk upon the dry bottom. All night we are crossing, for we are a great and numerous people, a mixed multitude. We go with our wives and husbands, our children, our pack animals, our livestock. All that is and all that will be Israel must pass through this ritual of immersion. We have descended into the *mikvah*, leaving behind forever our former lives of slavery, paganism and idol worship in Egypt. We are being baptized. We arise on the other side as free men, new creatures, every one of us born again.

Of course, Pharaoh tries to follow. Just before the first light of dawn, comes the final round in the contest of the gods. Is Pharaoh man enough… is Pharaoh god enough to keep the LORD from taking the Israelites away from him?

By the time the Egyptians realize that they cannot fight against the LORD, it is already too late. They turn to flee just as the first rays of the sun are spilling over the eastern horizon. It is too late. The waters crash over them. As the sun rises, we are a nation of free men and women standing on the shore of the sea. From our mouths, a mighty shout rises up to heaven.

The contest is over. God has made His point. He has established His reputation. There is none like Him. We sing, "Who is like You among the gods, O LORD? Who is like You, majestic in holiness, awesome in praises, working wonders?" (Exodus 15:1).

The contest is decided, the people are redeemed, and God has established His Name in the world. In the book of Deuteronomy, Moses sums up the entire Exodus episode:

> Has any god ever tried to take for Himself one nation out of another nation, by testings, by miraculous signs and wonders, by war, by a mighty hand and an outstretched arm, or by great and awesome deeds, like all the things the LORD your God did for you in Egypt before your very eyes? You were shown these things so that you might know that the LORD is God; besides Him there is no other. (Deuteronomy 4:34–35)

As a result of these great and awesome deeds, we stand on the opposite shore of the sea as a free people, a redeemed people. We are His people. The mixed multitude that went up from Egypt has been reborn as a free nation. We have all passed through the same immersion.

Fourteen hundred years or so later, the life of Yeshua was yet another round in the contest of the gods. Just as God sent Moses to work signs and wonders in order to bring the Israelites out of Egypt, Yeshua was sent with the same mission. God had sent Moses as a champion, a sort of incarnation to challenge Pharaoh. He made Moses like "God" to Pharaoh. Similarly, He sent Yeshua, the true incarnation, to work signs and wonders in order to draw the hearts of the people to God. In Egypt, a lamb was slain and its blood applied to the doorposts in order that the people chosen might be saved from the last plague, the final judgment. In the same way, on Passover 1400 years later, Yeshua died and His blood was applied as a mark and an atonement in order that the people chosen might be saved from final judgment. And just as the final redemption of the people did not occur until they went down into the sea and came back up on the other side, Yeshua in His resurrection has prepared that His chosen people might be immersed in His death and resurrection for eternal life.

We, the Redeemed, have been redeemed from slavery. In Romans 6, Paul likened our immersion into Messiah to a death and rebirth, borrowing heavily from the rubrics of the rabbinic conversion ritual via immersion. In 1 Corinthians he compared

Israel's passing through the Red Sea to an immersion ritual. This is narrative theology at work. Paul is thinking along the same historical/theological lines as he goes on to liken our new lives in Messiah to liberation from slavery. As he does so, he is obviously borrowing imagery from the Exodus as he describes our new lives in Messiah. In the following Romans 6 passage, he makes the case for why believers should live Torah lives.

> Don't you know that when you offer yourselves to someone (such as Pharaoh) to obey him as slaves, you are slaves to the one whom you obey—whether you are slaves to sin (Pharaoh and the Egyptians), which leads to death (drowning in the Red Sea or being skewered by a charioteer), or to obedience (to God), which leads to righteousness? But thanks be to God that, though you used to be slaves to sin (making bricks in Egypt), you wholeheartedly obeyed the form of teaching to which you were entrusted (you followed Moses out of Egypt).
>
> You have been set free from sin (i.e. passed through the Red Sea) and have become slaves to righteousness (God). I put this in human terms because you are weak in your natural selves (you still have a slave mentality). Just as you used to offer the parts of your body in slavery to impurity and to ever-increasing wickedness (i.e. brickmaking and temple building), so now offer them in slavery to righteousness (Torah and commandments) leading to holiness.
>
> When you were slaves to sin (Pharaoh's property), you were free from the control of righteousness (you didn't belong to God). What benefit did you reap at that time from the things you are now ashamed of? Those things result in death!
>
> But now that you have been set free from sin (crossed through the Red Sea) and have become slaves to God (on the other side of the Red Sea), the benefit you reap leads to holiness (you are free to serve God), and the result is eternal life. For the wages of sin is death (Egypt equals death), but the gift of God is eternal life in Messiah Yeshua our Lord. (Romans 6:16–23)

To Paul, our salvation in Yeshua is comparable to the Exodus of Israel from Egypt. Our re-creation in Messiah is comparable to Israel's passing through the Red Sea. However, Paul is not introducing anything that the Master had not taught already. It was Yeshua who compared the transformation of spirit to being "born again." It was Yeshua who told His disciples to henceforth celebrate Passover in remembrance of Him.

We are to keep the Passover in remembrance of this second and greater redemption.

This may work well for Jewish believers, but can Gentiles legitimately celebrate a Passover Seder? Can a Gentile "regard himself as though he personally had gone out of Egypt?" It would be foolish to imagine that the Master meant only for His Jewish disciples to keep the Feast. Surely, He did not mean for the Gentile disciples to be excluded from the table. As Paul addressed the mixed multitude in Corinth, he assumed that they were indeed keeping Passover.[13] After all, both Jew and Gentile had passed through the same great salvation. As Nicodemus learned, even Jews need to be born again in spirit. We need not be born again in the conventional sense of a conversion to Judaism, but in the sense of rebirth in Messiah. In Messiah, we have all experienced an Exodus from Egypt. All of us have passed through the sea.

We aren't the same. Everything is different now.

ENDNOTES

1 Exodus 12:48 does specify that "no uncircumcised male" may make a Passover sacrifice or eat of a Passover sacrifice. This prohibition applies equally to uncircumcised Jews and Gentiles. It does not, however, mean that an uncircumcised person cannot celebrate Passover or participate in the Seder or the Feast of Unleavened Bread. It is a prohibition specific only to sacrificing a Passover lamb and eating thereof, thus it is a non-factor outside of a Temple context.

2 1 Corinthians 5:7–8

3 Genesis 15:13

4 Genesis 50:24

5 Exodus 6:6–7

6 Exodus 7:1

7 Exodus 5:2

8 Exodus 12:38

9 Exodus 14:10

10 Exodus 14:11

11 Kaplan, 1995, pp. 320–323.

12 Probably Nakdimon ben Gurion of rabbinic lore.

13 1 Corinthians 5:7, 11:23–31

The Flock of Israel

7
The Flock of Israel
John 10

Some stories are so powerful that they seem to breathe a life of their own. They appear and reappear in different places and in different disguises. One such story is the famous *midrash* about Moses the shepherd. It reads as follows:

> Moses our teacher, peace be upon him, was tending the flock of Jethro in the wilderness when a little kid escaped from him. He ran after it until it reached a shady place... and the kid stopped to drink. When Moses approached it, he said, "I did not know you ran away because of thirst, you must be weary." So he placed the kid on his shoulder and walked away. Thereupon God said: "Because you have mercy in leading the flock of a mortal, you will surely tend my flock, Israel." (Shemot Rabbah 2:2)

Over and over again, Israel is compared to a flock. She is the flock of the Lord. Her leaders are her shepherds, appointed by her ultimate shepherd, the Lord Himself. "You led your people like a flock by the hand of Moses and Aaron,"[1] the Psalmist sings, "Hear us, O Shepherd of Israel, you who lead Joseph like a flock."[2]

Her greatest leaders were shepherds. Abraham, Isaac and Jacob were men with flocks. Jacob worked as a shepherd for Laban. Moses was a shepherd for Jethro. David was shepherd over his father's flocks. It is no surprise then that the Messiah of Israel should refer to Himself as "the good shepherd."

Yeshua retells the story of Moses and the lost sheep as a parable.[3] In the parable, He casts Himself in the role of Moses, seeking out the lost sheep of Israel. At one point in the Gospels, Yeshua even says, "I was sent only to the lost sheep of Israel."

But who are these lost sheep of Israel, and how do Gentile believers fit into that flock?

Three Parables

We find the story that Yeshua borrows from the *midrash* about Moses in Luke 15. In that story, Yeshua casts Himself as the shepherd who leaves the flock of ninety-nine sheep to pursue the one lost sheep and return it to the flock. He offers the story to us as one in a series of three thematically linked parables. They are the parable of the lost sheep (Luke 15:1–7), the parable of the lost coins (Luke 15:8–10) and the parable of the prodigal son (Luke 15:11–32).

Each of these three parables is linked by a common story, theme and meaning. The lost sheep correspond to the lost coin and to the prodigal son. The Shepherd that pursues the lost sheep corresponds to the woman searching for the coin and to the father waiting for his son's return. The ninety-nine other sheep correspond to the nine other coins and to the loyal but jealous son who did not leave home.

Yeshua tells the three parables of Luke 15 in response to a criticism raised in verses one and two of the chapter. He is criticized by the sages for eating with, associating with and even teaching "tax collectors and sinners." The sages charge that Yeshua is guilty by association. If He eats with sinners and fellowships with sinners and chooses sinners for His disciples, then He must be a sinner! It is an accusation that is leveled at the Master several times throughout the Gospels, and it is an understandable point of contention.

Throughout the ministry of the Master, He seemed to aim sharp criticisms at the religious and the faithful Jews while at the same time generously offering warmth, hospitality and gentle teaching to the irreligious and lawless of society. To the religious and observant Jews of the Master's day, it must have seemed as if Yeshua spurned those who strove to live lives according to God's instruction, while He coddled those who lived in open rebellion to God. He was a friend to tax collectors, harlots and sinners.

The Pharisees were at a loss to explain His seemingly irrational behavior. Here was a man who claimed to be a prophet of God, and more than a prophet, but rather than rebuking the sinners, He rebuked the righteous!

On one occasion (Luke 5), Yeshua attempted to explain His dualistic approach to ministry. He said, "It is not the healthy who need a doctor, but the sick. I have not come to call the righteous, but sinners to repentance." We should not read sarcasm into the Master's words. He genuinely meant what He said. He was not interested in the religious and righteous of Israel because, by comparison to the "sinners" of His day, they were not in need of repentance. He was concerned with the irreligious. He had not come to seek the righteous, but sinners.

This explains why Yeshua was sharply critical of the religious of His day. He regarded them as the healthy and the righteous of Israel. Therefore, He held them to a much higher standard and was quick to point out hypocrisy and pretense. His criticisms, however, were not a rejection of the religious. Rather, they were corrections.

On the other hand, when He was among the irreligious, He did not rebuke them as He did the Pharisees and teachers of Torah. The irreligious were outside of the domain of Torah. It does no good to rebuke someone for disobeying a law that they do not believe in. Therefore, He sought to first entice them to repent and return to obedience to the Father. He needed to bring them into the Kingdom before holding them up to the standards of the Kingdom.

However, the Pharisees and teachers of the Torah interpreted this behavior as hostility toward themselves and love for lawlessness. Therefore, they criticized Him saying, "He hangs out with bad company."

This is exactly the situation to which the parable triplet of Luke 15 is addressed.

Lost Sheep, Coins and Sons

In Luke 15 we read, "Now the tax collectors and 'sinners' were all gathering around to hear Him. But the Pharisees and the teachers of the law muttered, 'This man welcomes sinners and eats with them.'"[4]

Yeshua attempts to explain His mission to seek and save the lost of Israel by retelling the famous story of Moses seeking after the lost sheep. The Master tells the story this way. He says,

> Suppose one of you has a hundred sheep and loses one of them. Does he not leave the ninety-nine in the open country and go after the lost sheep until he finds it? And when he

> finds it, he joyfully puts it on his shoulders and goes home. Then he calls his friends and neighbors together and says, "Rejoice with me; I have found my lost sheep." I tell you that in the same way there will be more rejoicing in heaven over one sinner who repents than over ninety-nine righteous persons who do not need to repent.[5]

In the parable, the lost sheep of Israel are symbolic of the "sinners and tax collectors." The context makes that obvious. Yeshua is the shepherd like Moses. The ninety-nine remaining sheep are the righteous of Israel who don't need to repent (present company of Pharisees and teachers of the Torah included). Yeshua explains that just as the shepherd leaves the flock in order to pursue and rescue the one lost sheep, so too He leaves the religious and observant in order to pursue and rescue the irreligious and lawless of Israel.

In Luke 15, He goes on to tell the parable of the lost coins and then the parable of the prodigal son. The meaning of the three parables is the same. They are explanations of why the Master is seeking after the lost of Israel.

The prodigal son represents the "sinners and tax collectors." The faithful son represents the observant and religious of Israel. The father who goes to meet the prodigal and then prepares a banquet for him represents Yeshua who is pursuing the irreligious and lawless of Israel. He tells the parable to caricature the bitter attitude of the Pharisees and the teachers of the Torah toward those who are turning to repentance. Indeed, they are jealous just like the loyal son, because the Master seems to disregard them and spend all of His attention on these people of ill repute.

Each of these parables concludes with a scene of rejoicing. If there was any doubt about the meaning of the parables, Yeshua makes the meaning explicit in verse 7 when He says, "I tell you that in the same way there is more rejoicing in heaven over one sinner who repents than over ninety-nine righteous persons who do not need to repent."

Lost Jews or Lost Gentiles?

Unlike Torah, parables are not to be subjected to *midrashic* methods. Parables are not oracles. Quite the opposite. A parable is told to make a point clear and comprehensible. Parables are meant as illustrations and should be read as such. They are not allegories with multiple applications. They are told to make a singular point.[6]

The actual meaning of these three parables is obvious enough when they are read within the context of Luke 15. The context dictates the meaning. The lost sheep, the lost coin and the prodigal son all represent Jews who have strayed from the covenant norms and are regarded by the religious of their day as "sinners and tax collectors." In fact, they are sinners and tax collectors, but they are still Jews.

The Master Himself describes His ministry in these terms. When Zacchaeus the tax collector repents, Yeshua says, "Today salvation has come to this house, because this man, too, is a son of Abraham. For the Son of Man came to seek and to save what was lost."

The lost sheep of Israel are all Jews. They are the sinners and the backslidden among the Jewish people of the day.

The Master Himself makes this clear when He sends His disciples out to preach the Kingdom of Heaven in Matthew 10. In that passage, He tells His disciples, "Do not go among the Gentiles or enter any town of the Samaritans. Go rather to the lost sheep of Israel."[7]

We should also remember the occasion when Yeshua was approached by a Gentile woman in Matthew 15. He refused to speak to her. His disciples entreated Him to do something about her situation, but He replied, "I was sent only to the lost sheep of Israel."[8] In the Master's estimation, a Gentile woman does not qualify as being a "lost sheep of Israel."

Who are the lost sheep of Israel that Yeshua sought? They are clearly not Gentiles or even to be found among the Gentiles. They are not the Ten Lost Tribes. They are the sinners and the tax collectors, the backsliders and the irreligious of the Master's countrymen. They are the Jewish people. The meaning of the parable is patently clear.

Yeshua came to seek and save sinners. Jewish sinners.

Why am I belaboring an obvious point? Because it is possible that the Master's seemingly exclusive particularity might sometimes make non-Jews feel like second-class citizens in the

Kingdom. The Master's teaching regarding Gentiles would have been Paul's primary source of information while weighing the implications of the Mystery of the Gospel. Therefore, it is an important piece to the puzzle.

Second-Class Citizens

Ever since the days of the Gospel, the question of Gentile participation in Israel has haunted theology, and many dark musings have arisen from the words of Yeshua Himself.

When Yeshua says things like, "Do not go among the Gentiles, but only to the lost sheep of Israel," and when He says things such as, "I was sent only to the lost sheep of Israel," we Gentile followers of Yeshua are left feeling a little bit insecure. It seems as if the Master has no interest in us or as if we are second-class citizens in the Kingdom. It is disturbing to think that if we had been alive in the Master's day, He may have passed us by on the basis that we were Gentiles. It is unnerving to imagine.

Therefore, it might be very attractive to imagine that we are actually not Gentiles, but the long lost descendents of Israel—indeed, the very Lost Sheep of Israel that Yeshua came to seek and save. Or perhaps we may consider converting to Judaism, as if we could somehow join ourselves to that special flock of the LORD. If we are actually Israelites, then we are in the spotlight of the Gospels and at the center of the Master's concern and attention. Suddenly we would be able to regard ourselves as first-class citizens.

If we could discover that we were actually Jewish, or Israelite, or make a conversion to Judaism, then we would no longer feel awkward or hesitant about our participation in a Torah community or Messianic synagogue. We would no longer question our desire to live a Torah life. We would not feel self-conscious about wearing a tallit, or a kippa, or affixing a *mezuzah* to our door, because we would be Gentiles no more. Rather, we would be the lost sheep of Israel.

A Place at the Table

While it is true that the Master focused on His expressed intent to seek and save the lost sheep of Israel, He was often confronted with Gentiles vying for His attention. We never see a single instance in the Gospels where Yeshua does not ultimately meet the Gentile's request. Let's consider the first such occasion as an example.

The first Gospel instance of Yeshua encountering a Gentile in need is the story of the centurion with the sick and dying servant. The story is set in Capernaum. In the story, a certain Roman centurion has a dear servant who is sick and dying. He hears of Yeshua and entreats the elders of the synagogue to go and appeal to Yeshua on his behalf. The elders come to Yeshua and say: "This man deserves to have you do this, because he loves our nation and has built our synagogue."[9]

Like many non-Jews in the Hebrew Roots movement today, the centurion had a heart for Israel and the Jewish people. The elders testify, "He loves our nation." Surely this is a man with a "Jewish heart." Much like ourselves, he is certainly involved in the synagogue and is drawn to things Jewish. I would warrant he had a *mezuzah* on his door.

Yeshua complies with the request of the elders and sets out for the centurion's house. Yet before He arrives, the centurion sends word and says, "Master, don't trouble yourself, for I do not deserve to have you come under my roof." As a student of Jewish culture, the man was probably aware of the purity issues involved with Jews entering the house of a Gentile.[10] Yeshua Himself was not so concerned with the purity issues. He had already set out with the intent of entering the man's house and healing his servant.

The centurion, however, rather than inconvenience the Master, tells him, "But say the word, and my servant will be healed."

Yeshua is so impressed with the man's demonstration of faith that He says, "I tell you, I have not found such great faith even in Israel."

Yeshua is impressed with the faith of a Gentile.

Matthew's version of the story continues with Yeshua saying, "I say to you that many will come from the east and the west, and will take their places at the feast with Abraham, Isaac and Jacob in the kingdom of heaven. But the subjects of the kingdom will be thrown outside, into the darkness, where there will be weeping and gnashing of teeth."[11]

This is a hard saying. In this saying, the many who will come from the east and the west are Gentiles like the centurion. He and his faith are contrasted against the faithlessness of Israel.

Those who come to be seated are Gentiles. Those who are cast out are Israelites.

This is a hard saying because it seems to play into the hand of replacement theology. However, it does not mean that all Israel will be rejected and replaced by Gentiles.

The banquet prophecy is close to Paul's olive tree analogy. In that passage, some branches are broken off so that wild branches may be grafted in. So too with the Feast in the World to Come. Unworthy elements of Israel are sent from the table in order to make room for Gentiles to sit down.

In a rabbinic context, Yeshua's words are shocking. The Feast with Abraham, Isaac and Jacob is a well-known fixture in Jewish eschatology. However, in that eschatology, it is always Israel seated at the table with the Patriarchs, while the Gentiles are described as "the wicked." They are envisioned outside of paradise, hungry and in torment. In Yeshua's version of the story, the criterion for sitting at the table is faith, not ethnicity.

Being seated at the table with Abraham, Isaac and Jacob is not second-class citizenship. The Master clearly regards Gentiles as legitimate citizens in the Kingdom of Heaven, seated at the table of the righteous. Even seated with the Fathers! To be seated with the Fathers, one is certainly part of the family. Those Gentiles brought from the east and the west were not Israel, but they have been seated with Israel, and thus have become a part of Israel.

When Yeshua says this, He assigns Gentiles of faith the highest possible honor accorded to anyone in the whole of the Kingdom of Heaven. From His perspective, there is no cause for a Gentile inferiority complex. The Gentiles of faith will sit at the table of Abraham, Isaac and Jacob, the table of Israel, together with Israel.

This saying also explains the Master's ambiguity toward Gentiles and His passion for the "lost sheep of Israel." Because He foresaw the Gentile inclusion in Israel that was coming, He was all the more passionate for the sinners and tax collectors among His own people—lest they be sent from the table, thrown outside the kingdom and into outer darkness. The picture of Yeshua in the Gospels is the picture of a man on a rescue mission. He holds no disdain for Gentiles; rather He is racing against time for the souls of His own people.

Regarding those sent from the table, Paul reminds us, "And if they do not persist in unbelief, they will be grafted in, for God is able to graft them in again."[12] There is no lack of seats at God's table.

One Flock of Israel

In the parables of John chapter 10, Yeshua further illustrates His concept of the Gentile inclusion in Israel. In those passages, He returns to the flock metaphors employed in the synoptic Gospels. Again, He is the shepherd and Israel is the flock. He speaks of guarding the flock, leading the flock and even laying His life down for the flock. He is speaking of His relationship to His people Israel.

But then in verse 16 He introduces sheep from another flock. He says, "I have other sheep that are not of this sheep pen. I must bring them also. They too will listen to my voice, and there shall be one flock and one shepherd."

In the John passage, the sheep being gathered and joined to the already existing flock under one shepherd are Gentiles. Notice that they are not of the flock of Israel. They are "not of this sheep pen."

Sheep that are not part of the flock of Israel and not from the sheep pen (the land) of Israel are Gentiles. This is good news for Gentiles looking for a place among Israel. Notice that the Master does not say, "There shall be two flocks." Rather, there will be one flock; and it is the Gentiles who are joined to the flock of Israel, not vice versa. In the parable, Yeshua leads the Gentiles into the flock of Israel. Again, the Master does not assign Gentiles second-place status, nor does He separate them from Israelites. They are all to be in one flock, with one shepherd. The Gentiles are not second-class citizens. They have a full participation in the flock of Israel because the Good Shepherd joins them to the flock of Israel.

The Master did not have an anti-Gentile bias. From the beginning of His ministry, He was speaking of Gentiles of faith coming into the Kingdom and being seated at the table with Abraham, Isaac and Jacob. By saying this, He assigned them a place with the righteous of Israel. In every encounter He has with Gentiles, He complies with their requests. He envisions a day when He will lead the Gentiles like a flock of sheep and join them to the flock of Israel. From the Master's perspective, Gentiles of faith are to be identified with Israel and in Israel.

It is no surprise, then, that when Yeshua delivers the Great Commission to His disciples He tells them, "Go and make disciples of all nations (Gentiles), baptizing them in the name of the Father and of the Son and of the Holy Spirit, and teaching them to obey everything I have commanded you."

The Great Commission

During the term of His ministry, the Master focused His efforts and the efforts of His disciples on "the lost sheep of Israel." This was an urgent rescue mission, an attempt to restore the lawless (those who had strayed from Torah) of Israel to a saving faith before the doors of the Kingdom would be opened to the Gentiles. At the completion of His ministry and just prior to His ascension, He lifts the ban on teaching the Gospel to Gentiles. Instead, He tells His disciples, "Go and make disciples of all nations (Gentiles), immersing them in the name of the Father and of the Son and of the Holy Spirit, and teaching them to obey everything I have commanded you."

Often times, we Gentiles in Torah communities and in the Hebrew Roots movement are left wondering if we really have a right to practice Torah. We feel that the Shabbat, the Festivals, the laws of kosher, and all the things of Torah, are really meant for the Jews and "real Israelites." By observing Torah and practicing the commandments, it seems we are co-opting someone else's culture. This feeling of discomfort compels us to find some rationalization for our love of Torah and our desire to keep the commandments.

But why should we look any further than the Master?

The commandment to immerse the nations is evocative of the rabbinical conversion ritual. As we have learned in previous chapters, when a Gentile (that is, one from the nations) wants to convert to Judaism, he must pass through a ritual immersion. Subsequent to his immersion, he is regarded as an Israelite in every respect, and he is required to live a life obedient to the laws of Torah. Yeshua takes the same model and adopts it for His purposes. He commands His disciples to immerse the nations in His Name! Just as Paul will later co-opt the rubrics of the rabbinical conversion ritual to describe the New Creation that results from faith in Messiah, the Master co-opts the very ritual itself and commands His disciples to immerse the nations into His Name. There is a conversion implied here. Not a rabbinically formulated conversion where one metamorphoses from a Gentile into a Jew, but a no less stunning conversion takes place as we enter the flock of the Good Shepherd.

In the rabbinic ritual, the proselyte is required to live a life obedient to the laws of Torah subsequent to his immersion. Yeshua told His disciples, "Immerse them... teaching them to obey everything I have commanded you." Those are His words and His instruction for us non-Jews. We are to obey everything that He commanded His disciples because we are to be disciples too. Our immersion into Yeshua is a conversion of sorts. It does not make us Jewish, but it does make us disciples. Jew or Gentile, Israelite or not, discipleship to Yeshua is our highest calling.

One of the things that the Master commanded His disciples to do was to keep the commandments of Torah.[13] Therefore, we Gentile disciples are also to obey His command. Just as the disciples were commanded by Yeshua to obey the Torah, so too are we. We need look no further for an explanation of our desire to walk according to Torah. We need seek no other justification for keeping Sabbath or the Festivals or the kosher laws or any of the commands of Torah. We are disciples of Yeshua just as Peter, Andrew, James and John were disciples of Yeshua. Discipleship implies imitation. It is our job as disciples to imitate Messiah, and part of the imitation of Messiah is following the Torah.

The Torah is for all of Israel. Even for the Gentiles grafted into Israel.

In 1 Peter 2:25, the disciple Peter writes to his non-Jewish readers saying, "For you were like sheep going astray, but now you have returned to the Shepherd and Overseer of your souls." The Shepherd and Overseer of our souls so loved us that He left the other ninety-nine, picked us each up individually and carried us to His flock, joining us to His flock Israel.

There is only one flock. There is only one shepherd.

ENDNOTES

1 Psalm 77:20

2 Psalm 80:1

3 As is so often the case when comparing the word of Yeshua and rabbinic literature, we do not actually know whether the rabbinic version or the Gospel version is the older. Certainly the Gospel manuscripts are older than the written *midrash*, but the oral tradition behind a story like this might be very long. We can only be certain one version is dependent upon the other, but we don't know which is first.

4 Luke 15:1, 2

5 Luke 15:4–6

6 See Brad Young's (1998) *The Parables: Jewish Tradition and Christian Interpretation.*

7 Matthew 10:5, 6. This is contrary to Two House Theology. By virtue of elimination, Matthew 10:5, 6 disqualifies Gentiles (and even those who might only appear to be Gentiles) and Samaritans from being regarded as "lost sheep of Israel." If it actually was the Lost Tribes of Israel that the Master meant for His disciples to go to, then He should have sent His disciples to the Gentiles and the Samaritans. The Samaritans, even by the biblical record, are interbred with the Lost Tribes. Instead He sends them only to the Jews who know that they are Jews.

8 Matthew 15:24

9 Luke 7:4, 5

10 See John 18:28 and Acts 10:28 and Oholot 18:7.

11 Matthew 8:11, 12

12 Romans 11:23

13 Implicitly throughout his ministry, explicitly in Matthew 5:17–20.

Voices in the Thunder

8

Voices in the Thunder

Exodus 19, Acts 2

To be Israel is to be chosen. To imply that people outside of the chosen people are also chosen is confusing. If Gentiles are made joint heirs with Israel, does this not make the Gentiles also chosen? It was one of the things that Paul needed to sort through in his investigation of the mystery of the Gospel. To consider the matter, Paul must have rolled the scroll forward to Exodus 19, the story of how Israel became God's chosen people.

It happened at Mount Sinai. The sages of Israel refer to chapter 19 of Exodus as "the Betrothal at Sinai." The picture is a simple one. The people of Israel are the object of God's affection. He is the suitor, asking for her hand in marriage. He is to be their God. They are to be His people.

The romance actually began whilst still in Egypt. There the LORD had declared to Israel, "I will take you for my people, and I will be your God."[1] The expression, "You will be my people and I will be your God" is close to a legal formula from the sphere of marriage. In marriages of the Ancient Near East, the groom declared, "You will be my wife and I will be your husband."[2] In a sense, it is as if God has declared His intention to marry the people of Israel.

Moses brings them out of Egypt and to Mount Sinai for the big wedding. Moses, in his role as liaison between God and the people, is sometimes described as the "Friend of the Bridegroom."[3] In Jewish wedding customs, the friend of the bridegroom was the intermediary between the couple. It was the friend's job to present the bride to the groom. Moses filled this role by leading the people to Mount Sinai, and conducting the negotiations between God and Israel. When at last the LORD descended on Mount Sinai, Moses led the people out of the camp and to the foot of the mountain, presenting them to God.

The giving of the Law at Mount Sinai is described in Jewish literature as a betrothal and a wedding. Within the *midrash*, there are several short parables, which develop this theme. They all follow the same basic construction: A princess (Israel) is captured by bandits (Egypt). A King (God) happens along, sees the princess in distress, and rescues her. He then takes her to his palace (Mt. Sinai) and asks her to marry him. That's the basic layout of the imagery. There are variations. In one passage, Mount Sinai is compared to a wedding canopy. In another, the two stone tablets are referred to as the wedding contract.

The Exodus 19 betrothal is one of the most beautiful passages in the scriptures. If we might anthropomorphize the Holy One, blessed be He, the scene can best be illustrated as if God is on one knee before the young girl Israel, taking her hand in His, locking His eyes with hers and imploring her, "Will you marry me?"

Here's how God poses the question:

You yourselves have seen what I did to Egypt,
And how I carried you on eagles' wings
And brought you to myself.
Now if you will really hear my voice
And keep my covenant,
Then out of all nations you will be my treasured possession.
Although the whole earth is mine,
You will be for me a kingdom of priests and a holy nation.
(Exodus 19:4–6)

Israel responds: "We will do everything the LORD has said."

The girl said "yes," and the engagement ring is on her finger. But in actuality, getting engaged was not quite as simple as I am drawing it here. In the Ancient Near East, the betrothal of a woman was a formal affair. It entailed written contract agreements. In these written agreements, all the terms and conditions were stated. The responsibilities of both parties were spelled out clearly. What will be the bride price? What will be the dowry? What will the responsibilities of the bride entail? What must the groom do? What are his obligations as a husband? What are the bride's obligations as a wife? When will the wedding occur? All possible contingencies are addressed. It is a contract. It is a covenant.

A covenant is an agreement specifying terms and conditions incumbent upon both parties. It is a list of obligations, but it's more than a simple contract. A covenant is the definition of a relationship between two parties. In the ancient culture of the Bible, a covenant's terms and conditions were regarded as being inviolable.

In Exodus 19, God asks Israel to enter into a covenant relationship with Him. For His part, He offers to make Israel His "treasured possession, a kingdom of priests, a holy nation." He offers to make them into the People of God. For Israel's part of the deal, her responsibility is to "hear God's voice," and keep the terms of His covenant.

His covenant is the Torah. Israel's acceptance of the terms and conditions of the Torah qualifies her as the People of God.

Even before hearing the actual terms and conditions, Israel agrees. The people responded by saying, "All that the LORD has spoken we will do." It is as if God has requested Israel's hand in marriage and she has consented. She has agreed to be His special, intimate people; His *am segullah*.

No Other Nation

Within the Church, we Christians often refer to ourselves as the bride. However, the Torah, and all the Scriptures, seem clear that Israel is the promised bride. Can there be two brides? Is God a polygamist?

One legend about the giving of the Torah at Mount Sinai says that before God gave the Torah to Israel, He first offered it to all the other nations on earth. Each nation asked to hear the terms involved. Edom could not tolerate a law prohibiting murder. The Ishmaelites could not abide a commandment prohibiting theft. The Ammonites would have nothing to do with a law against immorality. For one reason or another, each nation on earth rejected the Torah. In Exodus 19, however, even before Israel had heard the laws and stipulations of this covenant proposal they said, "We will do everything the LORD has said." Therefore, the Torah was given to Israel, and through the covenant at Sinai, Israel became the People of God.

To our modern and pluralistic sensibilities, the idea of a singular People of God seems very narrow and ethnocentric.

Why would God choose one people above all others? Why are the Jews the Chosen People? Theologians call this seemingly unfair conundrum the "scandal of particularity." Call it what we will, the Bible is very clear on this point. Out of all the peoples on the earth, out of all the nations, God has entered into covenant with only one people, only one nation. That nation is Israel. God did not call the Swedes to Mount Sinai. The Irish are not a kingdom of priests. The Italians are not a holy nation. The French are not the People of God. The Americans are not the Chosen People.

We should go a step further and point out that God did not call the Baptists to Mount Sinai. The Catholics are not a kingdom of priests. The Lutherans are not a holy nation. The Presbyterians are not the People of God. The Evangelicals are not the Chosen People.

God has not made a covenant with any other people on the earth. There is no other nation born by Him. If non-Jews want to be a part of the People of God, we have to leave our people and join ourselves to Israel. God has made a covenant with no other nation.

Where then does this leave the Gentiles? Paul says that Gentiles are "excluded from citizenship in Israel and foreigners to the covenants of the promise, without hope and without God in the world."[4] Is this fair? Perhaps not. But God has never played by the rules of men. If He desired to take a single nation for Himself, to the exclusion of all other nations, then that is His business. He is, after all, God.

Israel alone, among all the peoples of the earth, enjoys a relationship with the Creator. If the Gentile wants to enter into covenant relationship with the God of Israel, he must enter into the nation of Israel. Another way of saying this is that if the Gentile wants to be saved, he must join the covenant God has made with Israel. How do we enter this covenant? The same way Israel entered the covenant. She entered by agreeing to "hear" God's voice.

Yeshua invokes the Mount Sinai covenant imagery when He speaks of the Gentile inclusion. In John 10:16 He says, "I have other sheep that are not of this sheep pen. I must bring them also. They too will hear my voice, and there shall be one flock and one shepherd." Notice that there is only one flock, and participation in the flock is based upon listening to the shepherd's voice.

How did Israel become the People of God? How did she become the bride? She did it by agreeing to the terms of His covenant. By agreeing to hear His voice.

God is not a polygamist.

The Voices at Sinai

In the story of the giving of the Torah at Mount Sinai, Exodus 20:18 says, "And all the people saw the thunderings..."

The Hebrew text of Exodus 20:18 does not actually use the word thunder. Instead of thunder, the word *qolot* is employed. *Qolot* is the plural form of the Hebrew *qol*. *Qol* means "voice." So the Torah literally says, "And all the people saw the voices."

The word *qol* (voice) is used as a keyword device in this passage. It is repeated to artfully punctuate the text of Exodus 19 and 20. Let's look at how often and in how many ways the word *qol* is used in these passages.

The children of Israel are brought to Mount Sinai to receive an offer of covenant. Through Moses, the LORD tells the Children of Israel that if they will indeed "hear His *qol* (voice) and keep His covenant," then they will be His special treasure: His people. "Even though the whole world is mine," He tells them, "You will be for me a kingdom of priests and a holy nation."[5] The only contingency is that they must "hear God's Voice."

In Hebrew, "hearing someone's voice" is idiomatic for obedience. God is asking Israel for obedience. In order to be His unique and separate people, (indeed, to be His bride) Israel must live in obedience to God's voice. What is His voice? It is the commandments of the Torah, the terms and conditions of His marriage covenant with her.

Even before hearing the actual *qol* (voice) of God, Israel agrees. The people respond by saying, "All that the LORD has spoken we will do." It is as if God has requested Israel's hand in marriage and she has consented. She has agreed to be His special, intimate people.

Three days later, Israel encounters the voices at the mountain. Early in the morning, the cloud descends onto the mountain. There is thunder and lightning and the sound of the trumpet (*shofar*). Literally translating from Exodus 19:16 we read, "...and there were *qolot* (voices) and lightnings, and a heavy cloud upon the mountain, and an exceedingly strong *qol* (voice) of a *shofar*; and all the people in the camp trembled."

The revelation of God at Mount Sinai commences with voices, presumably thunder, accompanied by lightning, and the loud voice of the *shofar*. These voices crescendo into verse 19 where it says, "And the *qol* (voice) of the *shofar* was growing, and exceedingly strong! And Moses spoke, and God answered him in a *qol* (voice)."

All the people heard the voice of God as He spoke the Ten Commandments recorded in chapter 20. It was an unprecedented and not to be repeated moment in the history of the universe. An entire nation literally heard the voice of God speaking. They did not hear God in an ethereal or quasi-spiritual sense. Rather, they audibly heard the voice of God speaking. It was a vivid dramatization of the idiom employed at the beginning of the story, "If you will indeed hear my *qol* (voice)."

Seventy Voices

By the time we come to Exodus 20:18, "And all the people saw the voices," we have already learned that the voices are the voice of God.

Most translations smooth out the Hebrew of verse 18 by translating the word "voices" as thunder. Thunder agrees with the context of the thunder and lightning at Mount Sinai. The sages of the *midrash*, however, read the passage literally, without our glosses. Based upon their literal reading of the Hebrew, they derived a legend about the voices of God at Mount Sinai. In the *Midrash Rabbah*, Rabbi Yochanan wonders about the implications of God revealing Himself in a multitude of voices.

"The Torah says, 'And all the people saw the voices.' Note that it does not say 'the voice,' but 'the voices'; wherefore R. Yochanan said that God's voice, as it was uttered, split up into seventy voices, in seventy languages, so that all the nations should understand" (Shemot Rabbah 5:9).

The Talmud also quotes Rabbi Yochanan's tradition of the seventy voices at Mount Sinai. In the Talmudic version, Rabbi Yochanan is explaining a verse from Psalm 68. The verse reads, "The LORD announced the Word, and great was the company of those who proclaimed it."[6] Rabbi Yochanan explains the great company of proclaimers to be the multifaceted voice of God that speaks in the seventy languages:

"Rabbi Yochanan said: 'What is meant by the verse, "The Lord announced the word, and great was the company of those who proclaimed it."?—Every single word that went forth from the Omnipotent was split up into seventy languages'" (Shabbat 88b).

What does Rabbi Yochanan mean? In the world of rabbinic thought and literature, all of humanity is divided into seventy families of mankind. The number is derived from the seventy descendants of Noah's sons in Genesis 10. Talmudic literature frequently speaks of the seventy nations, meaning all nations. The seventy nations are to be understood as idiomatic for all mankind.

At Babel, each family of man was given a language. When the sages speak of the seventy languages, it is to be understood as all languages.

What Rabbi Yochanon is telling us is that as God spoke the words of Torah at Mount Sinai, His voice spoke simultaneously in all the languages of the world. Why? So that all mankind might hear and receive the Torah in their own language. The Torah is meant to have universal appeal. It is an open invitation to all mankind. The Torah is offered to anyone who will "hear God's voice and keep His covenant." Anyone can be part of the marriage. Anyone can join the bride.

Another legend has it that the Torah was given in the wilderness, which belonged to no particular nation, so that all nations could have access to it. There is a deep universalism implied here.

Only Israel was able to enter into covenant with God and become the People of God. Israel alone is a kingdom of priests and God's holy people. However, the invitation to Israel's covenant is left wide open to all mankind.

The legend of the Torah in seventy languages appears again at Mount Ebal. In Deuteronomy 27, Moses commands Israel to erect an altar on Mount Ebal. They are to build an altar as part of a covenant renewal ceremony. They are to plaster over the stones of the altar and write all the words of the Torah "very clearly" upon the altar. In Joshua 8, the Children of Israel arrive at Shechem and build the altar on Mount Ebal as Moses commanded them.

The *Mishnah* records the details of the ceremony. In the *Mishnah*, we read that the Israelites wrote out the whole Torah in seventy languages on the altar. "They brought the stones and built the Altar and plastered it with lime. Then they wrote on it all the words of the Torah in seventy tongues, as it is written, 'very clearly.'"[7]

When the Hebrew Scriptures were translated into Greek, the Greek Bible was called the "Seventy" (Septuagint). Again, the image is of the Torah going forth in all tongues. How are we to understand this idea?

When God offered the Torah to Israel, He offered it as the terms by which Israel could become His bride, His special treasure. "If you will hear my *qol* (voice) and keep my covenant, then out of all nations you will be my treasured possession. Although the whole earth is mine, you will be for me a kingdom of priests and a holy nation."[8]

However, the offer made to Israel does not exclude non-Israelites. Anyone from any nation who will hear God's voice and keep His covenant will be included in this relationship. Anyone who responds to God's invitation to covenant relationship is welcome to join the peculiar people and take a place among the kingdom of priests.

Judaism does not hold the copyright on the Torah. Paul reasons it out in the book of Romans by asking us, "Is God the God of Jews only? Is He not the God of Gentiles too?"[9] Clearly, He is the God of the Gentiles too. Therefore, His Torah is an open invitation to the whole world.

The Voice of Fire

In Exodus 19 and 20, God steps down onto Mount Sinai. He speaks the Ten Commandments in the hearing of all the people. At the end of the narrative we read, "And all the people saw the voices and the torches."

We would normally smooth out the Hebrew of verse 18 by translating the word "saw" as "heard," and by translating the word "torches" as "lightning." Thus, we can paraphrase, "And all the people heard the thunder and saw the lightning." The sages, however, read the passage literally, without our glosses. Based upon their literal reading of the Hebrew, the people saw voices and torches.

What does it mean, "the people saw voices"? How does one see a sound? How does one see a voice? Where did the torches come from? What are they?

In Deuteronomy, Moses retells the story of hearing God's voice at Sinai. In ten different passages, he reminds Israel that they heard God's voice speak to them "from out of the fire." Repeatedly he says, "You all heard the voice speaking from out of the fire."

Regarding this fiery voice of God, the disciples of Rabbi Ishmael applied a verse from Jeremiah. The verse says, "'Is not my word like fire,' declares the LORD, 'and like a hammer that breaks a rock in pieces?'"[10]

How is God's word like fire? How is His word like a hammer? In explaining this verse, the disciples of Rabbi Ishmael vividly imagined God's voice at Mount Sinai to be like a sledgehammer breaking up large stones. With each successive blow a multitude of fiery sparks are scattered in every direction.

"The School of R. Ishmael taught the meaning of the verse: 'and like a hammer that breaks a rock in pieces,' just as a hammer is divided into many sparks, so too every single word that went forth from the Holy One, blessed be He, split up into seventy languages" (Shabbat 88b).

According to their reading, the voice of God at Mount Sinai not only split into seventy voices speaking seventy different tongues, but those voices were like hot sparks flying forth from a hammer's blows on stone.

Is not His word like fire? The sages of the *midrash* thought so. According to their interpretation of Exodus 20:18, all the people really did see the voice of God, and torches too, because the voice of God appeared to them like hot, burning torches! As He spoke, His words took shape as torches of fire.

Consider the following passage from an anthology of such legends called *The Midrash Says*:

"On the occasion of [the giving of] the Torah, the [Children of Israel] not only heard the LORD's voice, but actually saw the sound waves as they emerged from the LORD's mouth. They visualized them as a fiery substance. Each commandment that left the

Lord's mouth traveled around the entire camp and then came back to every Jew individually..."[11]

These are some of the stories of Mount Sinai. At Mount Sinai, the Lord told Israel, "If you will hear my voice... you will be for me a kingdom of priests and a holy nation." Israel not only heard the voice of God at Mount Sinai, they heard it in every language. They saw it too! His voice came to them as fire.

The Voice of Pentecost

Another ancient Jewish tradition about the Giving of the Torah at Mount Sinai has to do with the timing of the event. Judaism regards the festival of Shavuot (Pentecost) to be the anniversary of the day on which God spoke at Sinai. The festival is celebrated as the Festival of the Giving of the Torah. In the synagogue, a wedding contract between God and Israel is read on Shavuot. The Torah is dressed in white like a bride's gown on Shavuot. The whole congregation recites the Ten Commandments together on Shavuot. Exodus chapters 19 and 20 are publicly read on Shavuot. Pentecost (Shavuot) is the day the Giving of the Torah is remembered and re-enacted. It is celebrated as a wedding anniversary for God and His bride.

Therefore, the Feast of Shavuot, in Jewish tradition, is also the anniversary of the day when God's voice spoke in all languages of the world and was visible as torches of fire which came "to every Jew individually."

In Acts chapter 2, Shimon Peter and the other disciples were gathered to celebrate this "Wedding Anniversary." They were gathered together to celebrate the festival of Pentecost when the Holy Spirit fell upon them in the form of tongues of fire. These torches of fire came to rest on each individual disciple. As a literary device and as genuine supernatural phenomenon, the miracle is a clear allusion to the legend of God's fiery voice at Mount Sinai. In addition, subsequent to receiving this fiery spirit, the disciples find themselves proclaiming the Gospel in every language. The miracle of speaking in all tongues is another definite allusion to the giving of the Torah at Mount Sinai. It is a literal fulfillment of the Psalm later quoted by Rabbi Yochanan, "The Lord announced the word, and great was the company of those who proclaimed it."

Whether or not the tradition of the seventy languages at Sinai and the fiery words at Sinai preserve actual historical memories of the Mount Sinai experience is not of great consequence. It is consequential, however, to remember that Shimon Peter and the disciples and followers of Yeshua were all well aware of the Shavuot legends. We can only assume that those legends predate the book of Acts, otherwise the allusions would be lost. Thus, they must have known the story of the giving of the Torah on Shavuot. They knew the story of the words of fire resting on each individual on Shavuot. They knew the story of God's voice speaking to all mankind in every language on Shavuot. Therefore, the miracles, signs and wonders that came upon them in Acts chapter two carried deep significance. The tongues of fire and the speaking in every tongue were both direct allusions to the Mount Sinai wedding experience and the receiving of the Torah. God was certainly underscoring the inseparable relationship between His Holy Spirit and His Holy Torah!

A Voice to the Jews

As Shimon Peter and the other believers that were gathered on that fateful Pentecost began to preach the Gospel, their words were uttered in every language. Jews from all over the world were present in Jerusalem to celebrate the Feast of Pentecost. Luke lists fifteen different place names and nations from which they had come. Each person heard the Gospel being proclaimed in his own native tongue.

However, Luke is careful to point out to us that those assembled there that day were all Jews. He prefaces his description of the event by saying, "And there were dwelling at Jerusalem Jews, devout men, out of every nation under heaven."[12] They are devout Jews from a variety of locales. They represent the wide diversity of the first century Diaspora. But they are all Jews, or at the very least, proselytes to Judaism. Even the "strangers from Rome" in vs. 10 are described as "both Jews and proselytes."

As Peter speaks to the crowd, he addresses them as "all Israel." The term "all Israel" is a common way of speaking of Diaspora Judaism even today. Peter's address is meant in that regard. His message is not just for those assembled, but also for all Jews (and Israelites) everywhere.

Undoubtedly there were also Gentiles present, God-fearers and the like, but they are not part of the story, nor are they part of Peter's address to "all Israel." Peter has not yet even considered the possibility of Gentile participation (short of conversion to Judaism).

Luke goes to some pains to make sure we understand that the faith is Jewish up through this point in his narrative. It is important for Luke to show us that the Gospel is received only by Jews because he is setting us up for the central conflict of the book of Acts. The central conflict of Acts (indeed, the dramatic theme of the whole book) is the controversy over the Gentile inclusion in the Kingdom. It is a controversy that does not erupt until Acts 10 and the conversion of Cornelius. Therefore, Luke is careful to point out that even though the new converts of Acts chapter 2 came from a variety of geographic locales, they were all Jews (whether by birth or by rabbinic conversion).

In subsequent chapters of Acts we meet the Ethiopian eunuch, but there is no reason to assume he wasn't Jewish. Ethiopian Jews are with us to this day. We also see Samaritan conversions, but even Samaritans are quasi-Israelites. They are not quite Gentiles. Not until Acts 10 are Gentile believers formally introduced into the mix.

A Voice to the Nations

After Shimon Peter takes the Gospel to Cornelius the Gentile and his household, he returns to a less than enthusiastic welcome among the Jewish believers in Jerusalem. "The apostles and the brothers throughout Judea heard that the Gentiles also had received the word of God. So when Peter went up to Jerusalem, the circumcised believers criticized him."[13] Shimon Peter finds himself in a defensive posture, explaining his radical decisions. It must have seemed radical even to him.

When he had arrived at Cornelius's house, he had said, "I now realize how true it is that God does not show favoritism but accepts men from every nation who fear Him and do what is right."[14] That kind of thinking was a dramatic reversal of Shimon Peter's theology. Prior to his vision of the sheet and the unclean animals,[15] Shimon Peter must have assumed that God certainly did show favoritism. After all, wasn't the nation of Israel God's special treasure, His kingdom of priests and His holy nation?

Cornelius and his household were not Jews. They weren't even Israelites. They were pure-blooded Gentiles without a claim or hope in Israel. Hence Peter refers to Cornelius as "one of another nation."[16] The term "one of another nation" makes it obvious that Cornelius was not an Israelite in any regard.

Prior to his vision, Shimon Peter must have assumed that the Gospel of Yeshua was meant only for Israel. He even intimates as much when he refers to the Gospel as the "message God sent to the people of Israel."[17] The people gathered in Cornelius's house are not the people of Israel. They are strangers to the covenant.

Imagine Shimon Peter's surprise. Imagine the surprise of the other Jews who had come with him. We read, "The circumcised believers who had come with Peter were astonished that the gift of the Holy Spirit had been poured out even on the Gentiles. For they heard them speaking in tongues..."[18]

The significance of the miracle could not have been lost on Shimon Peter. It was God's confirmation that the Gospel was also meant for the Gentiles. Just as the voice of God was split into the seventy languages of the Gentiles at Mount Sinai (according to the legends), just as the Jewish believers had spoken the Gospel in all the languages of the Nations at Pentecost, now the Gentiles in Cornelius's house were experiencing the same miracle. The voice of God was speaking in various languages to them and through them. They had not gone through a rabbinic conversion ritual. They were still Gentiles.

When Shimon Peter heard them speaking in the "seventy languages," he could no longer theologically exclude those Gentiles from Israel. They had heard the voice of God, just as Israel had heard it at Mount Sinai. They had heard the voice of God, and the promise was that anyone who heard His voice would be God's special treasure, a kingdom of priests and a holy people: Israel. That was the promise of the betrothal.

Confident in the definitive sign of the seventy languages, Shimon Peter cried out, "Can anyone keep these people from being baptized with water? They have received the Holy Spirit just as we have."[19]

The First Epistle of Peter

For Gentiles converting into Judaism according to the rabbinically prescribed ritual, immersion is supposed to follow circumcision. Circumcision is the sign of entering the covenant. Immersion is a symbolic death and rebirth. The Gentile going down into the water of immersion is said to die to his old Gentile self. As he emerged from the water, he is said to be "reborn" as a Jew. Recall that the term "born again" originally referred to this symbolic rebirth as a Jew.[20]

In rabbinic Judaism, one who has undergone a ritual conversion of circumcision and baptism is no longer referred to as a Gentile. He has been born again. He is a Jew and a full-blooded part of Israel.

In the case of Cornelius and his household, Shimon Peter took the almost unprecedented step of forgoing circumcision. I say almost unprecedented because there is a minority opinion in the Talmud that states one who is immersed, though not circumcised, is still regarded as an Israelite. Rabbi Yehoshua reasoned that if immersion was sufficient to mark a woman's conversion, it was sufficient for a man as well:

"If a man went through the prescribed immersion but had not been circumcised," Rabbi Yehoshua said, "Behold he is a proper proselyte; for so we find that the mothers (Sarah, Rivkah, Rachel and Leah) went through ritual immersion but had not been circumcised" (Yevamoth 46a).

For Peter, the evidence of the miraculous voices in every language was compelling enough. He needed no further convincing of the full covenant status of the Gentile believers. By virtue of their spontaneous Mount Sinai experience, they were as much entitled to the name "Israel" as he was.

The change in Shimon Peter's theology is evidenced in his first Epistle. 1 Peter is a book written to Gentile believers. In fact, one source indicates that the early church used to read 1 Peter to new converts on the day of their baptism.[21]

That the Gentile believers are the subjects of 1 Peter is clear from the outset. Peter contrasts their current state with "the evil desires you had when you lived in ignorance."[22] He reminds them "you were redeemed from the empty way of life handed down to you from your forefathers."

Peter also reminds his readers that in the past, they did "what Gentiles choose to do—living in debauchery, lust, drunkenness, orgies, carousing and detestable idolatry."[23] However, since their conversion, he no longer regards them as Gentiles. Instead, they are "God's Chosen, strangers in the world,"[24] the "born again."[25] They are like "new born babies."[26]

Peter points out to his readers that they are not included in God's household on the basis of their own bloodlines. They are not the natural seed of Abraham. Rather, they are part of the people of God on the basis of "an imperishable seed," planted in them "through the living and enduring word of God."[27] This means that the seed implanted in them is not implanted by means of sexual reproduction, as would be the case if it were a genetic reference. Rather, the seed implanted in them is by means of the power of the word of God.

As a result, they are no longer Gentiles. They are to live exemplary lives "among the Gentiles,"[28] but they themselves "are a chosen people, a royal priesthood, a holy nation, a people belonging to God."[29]

"Chosen people," "royal priesthood," "holy nation" and "people belonging to God" are all titles of Israel. They are the very roles God offered to Israel at Mount Sinai if only she would "hear His voice and keep His covenant." Now the Gentiles have heard that voice which offered the Torah in the seventy languages of the nations. They have entered that covenant, to keep it through the auspices of Yeshua. They have become a part of Israel the Bride.

As Gentile believers, we find our position in Israel spelled out here. We are no longer to be regarded as Gentiles. We are part of the People of God. We have become a "chosen people, a royal priesthood, a holy nation, a people belonging to God." We have been so made on the basis of an "imperishable seed" planted in us "through the living and enduring word of God," not a perishable seed inherited from distant ancestors. We have become a part of the people of Israel.

The People of God

In 1 Peter chapter 2, verse 10, Peter tells his readers, "Once you were not a people, but now you are the people of God; once you had not received mercy, but now you have received mercy." His words are borrowed from the prophet Hosea.

Hosea used a similar phrase to give hope to Israel in a time of apostasy. In the book of Hosea, the ten northern tribes had failed to keep God's covenant and had forgotten to hear His voice. Their disobedience had resulted in alienation from God. The LORD told them, "You are not my people, and I am not your God." He compared them to an unfaithful wife. The bride of God was to be divorced.

However, He did not leave them hopeless and dejected. Rather, He told them of a day of repentance, a day when they would return to Him. He said, "Yet the Israelites will be like the sand on the seashore, which cannot be measured or counted. In the place where it was said to them, 'You are not my people,' they will be called 'sons of the living God.'"

It is a prophecy of the ultimate reign of Messiah in the Kingdom to come.

Shimon Peter seized upon the image because it was deftly applicable to the Gentile converts to whom he was writing. The Gentiles, like Israel in the day of her apostasy, were previously alienated from God. They were not God's people. They did not know God's mercy. Now, like Israel in the future day of her repentance, the Gentiles had become "sons of the living God." Shimon declares to his Gentile converts, "Once you were not a people, but now you are the people of God; once you had not received mercy, but now you have received mercy."[30] Paul uses the same passage for the same purpose in Romans chapter 9.

As Peter wrote to them, he was transmitting the voice of God from Mount Sinai as it was split into the seventy languages of the nations. He was carrying out the commandment of his Master, "Therefore go and make disciples of all nations, baptizing them in the name of the Father and of the Son and of the Holy Spirit, and teaching them to obey everything I have commanded you."

ENDNOTES

1 Exodus 6:7

2 *Encyclopedia Judaica,* Vol. 5 "Covenant."

3 Pirke di Rabbi Eliezer 41. See also Exodus Rabbah 43:7, Numbers Rabbah 21:2, Deuteronomy Rabbah 1:2, 3:12. Compare John 3:29–30.

4 Ephesians 2:12

5 Exodus 19:5, 6

6 Psalm 68:11

7 *Mishnah* Sotah 7:5

8 Exodus 19:5, 6

9 Romans 3:29

10 Jeremiah 23:29

11 Weissman, Moshe. 1995. Shemos 182 citing *Midrash Chazit.*

12 Acts 2:5

13 Acts 11:1, 2

14 Acts 10:34

15 For a thorough explanation of the vision of the sheet see *Torah Club Volume 4* comments on Acts 10.

16 Acts 10:28

17 Acts 10:35

18 Acts 10:45, 46

19 Acts 10:47

20 Yevamoth 47b, 48b

21 See Tyndale's *Illustrated Bible Dictionary* Vol. 3 article on 1 Peter. We should point out that the early congregations were not exclusively Gentile or exclusively Jewish. Rather, they were synagogue-styled assemblies comprised of both Jewish and Gentile believers. Thus there were undoubtedly Jewish readers of Peter's epistles as well as Gentiles. However, the language of 1 Peter leans heavily toward addressing recent Gentile converts and introducing them to the new way of life they have entered.

22 1 Peter 1:14

23 1 Peter 4:3

24 1 Peter 1:1

25 1 Peter 1:23

26 1 Peter 2:2

27 1 Peter 1:23

28 1 Peter 2:12

29 1 Peter 2:9

30 Though Shimon Peter used these prophetic passages about the ten northern tribes metaphorically to speak of the Gentile inclusion, we must not forget that the Gentiles he was writing to were real Gentiles indeed. Shimon's readers were "former Gentiles" not "former Israelites." They were born of "imperishable seed" planted through "the word of God," not of natural seed born of Israelite descent. Their forefathers were not described as the noble patriarchs Abraham, Isaac and Jacob, but as pagans who handed on an "empty way of life." His readers were "reborn" not "returned." They were Gentiles from among the seventy nations of the world.

David's Fallen Sukkah

9
David's Fallen Sukkah
Acts 15

Jerusalem in the year 49 A.D.

The Council of the Elders has been convened. Seventy bearded Jews have crowded themselves into the hall and seated themselves in a half circle. Two more Jews are standing in front of them giving testimony. The elders are listening intently.

This is not the Sanhedrin, but like the Sanhedrin, these seventy men are legislators. Like the Sanhedrin, their word is the final authority. They are the highest court of appeal among the believers. The decisions these men implement are binding on all the congregations of believers.

Among these elders are several familiar faces. Most of them were among the seventy disciples of Yeshua. Some of them were even numbered among the Twelve. Isn't this one seated up close Yochanon ben Zavdai (John)? And the fellow with the parchments is certainly Mattityahu Levi (Matthew) the tax collector. Shimon Peter is, of course, present. There are others of the Twelve as well.

The president of the Council is none other than Yaakov HaTzaddik (James the Righteous), Yaakov ben Yoseif. He is James the brother of Yeshua, and he even bears some resemblance to Him. He is young to be at the head of such a venerable assembly, but over the years, he has won the confidence of his brother's disciples. The congregations of believers throughout the world look to the men of the Jerusalem Council for leadership and guidance, and the council, in turn, looks to Yaakov for the same.

The two men giving testimony are Shaul and Bar-Naba. They have come up from Antioch. They are reporting the results of their work among the Gentiles. Shaul cannot contain his zeal as he retells their adventures. His hands are waving and his beard is wagging as he talks. Everywhere they went, everywhere they preached, God was opening the door of faith to the Gentiles! The Gentiles in every city were turning to Yeshua. His obvious enthusiasm is contagious and smiles are spreading among the elders.

Then there is an interruption.

The Pharisees Object

Just as the testimony of Shaul and Bar-Naba is beginning, several of the elders stand to their feet, a dozen or more men. Like Shaul himself, these men are Pharisees. That much is obvious. They are Pharisees, but they are also zealous believers in Messiah and brothers in the Kingdom. They wait for Yaakov to give them permission to speak.

Yaakov acknowledges them and gives them the floor. Shaul and Bar-Naba sit down.

The spokesman for their group steps forward and addresses the council.

"Brothers," he charges, "The Gentile believers must be circumcised and required to obey the Torah of Moses."

What does he mean? He means that if a Gentile desires salvation and participation in the Kingdom, he must make a full and formal conversion to Judaism. According to this opinion, nothing less than a full conversion to Judaism will be adequate to ensure salvation. The charge has been made and the brother Pharisees return to their seats.

The elders debate the issue for hours. The arguments are heated and loud. Proof texts are cited to support the one side, and then more proofs are presented to support the other. "Have you not read?" "Is it not written?" "Have you never seen where it says?" Each opinion is backed with Scripture and full conviction. Each of the elders is convinced of the unassailable veracity of his own particular argument.

Notice that they aren't arguing about whether or not Gentiles should keep Torah. That isn't the question set before them. The question they are arguing is whether or not Gentiles must be circumcised in order to merit salvation. There is a world of difference between those two questions. Circumcision stands for the rabbinic conversion ritual, so the question is, "Must Gentiles convert to Judaism under the auspices of the rabbinically prescribed ritual in order to be saved?"

The objection of Paul's opponents is based upon the "theology of particularity" which characterizes Judaism. Israel alone is the chosen people! Israel alone is God's inheritance and special treasure! There is ample scripture to support such a notion. To even consider opening the door of particularity to any and every ethnicity is to compromise that select status. Uncircumcised Philistines in the Kingdom of Heaven, sitting at the table with Abraham, Isaac and Jacob? Unthinkable! Borderline blasphemy!

Shimon's Rebuttal

At long last, all the voices have been heard. Everyone has had a chance to say his piece, except for one lone elder. It is Shimon, who is called Peter.

Shimon Peter stands and takes the floor. "Brothers, you know that some time ago God made a choice among you that the Gentiles might hear from my lips the message of the Gospel and believe."

Everyone remembers the incident in Caesarea. Everyone remembers the debate that was sparked those many years ago when Shimon returned with word of the conversion of a Roman centurion and his whole family.

Shimon continues, "God, who knows the heart, showed that He accepted those Gentiles by giving the Holy Spirit to them, just as He did to us. He made no distinction between them and us, for He purified their hearts by faith. Now then, why do you try to test God by putting on the necks of the disciples a yoke that neither we nor our fathers have been able to bear? No! We believe it is through the grace of our Lord Yeshua that we are saved, just as they are."

Shimon's argument is simple. He points out that even Jews are not saved through their obedience to the Torah. If used as a means to attain salvation, the Torah would be an unbearable yoke. Generation after generation of Jewish history has already proven that all men sin and fall short of the glory of God. No one is saved through keeping the Torah. Instead, salvation for the Jewish believers comes through the grace of Yeshua. "Why would it be any different for Gentiles?" Shimon asks. Why indeed?

Furthermore, when the Pharisees speak of obeying "the whole Torah," they are speaking of much more than just the five books of Moses. The "whole Torah," or the "yoke of Torah," is idiomatic within rabbinical Judaism. It includes not only the written Torah, but also all of the Oral Torah, along with its traditions, fences and halachic rulings.[1] Everyone in attendance at the council understands full well what Peter means by referring to Torah as a "yoke that neither we nor our fathers have been able to bear."

Even by the first century, Torah observance had become a confusing maze of laws and traditions stacked upon commandments which the simple and uneducated found nearly impossible to navigate. Peter asks, "Do we really mean to saddle the Gentiles with the complexity and weight of Oral Law and tradition? Isn't faith in Yeshua adequate?" After all, Shimon Peter himself and the other core disciples of Yeshua were not scholars and sages, they were fishermen who ate bread before washing their hands and husked grain while walking through the fields on Shabbat. "Shall we then hold the Gentiles to a higher standard than we ourselves are beholden to?" Shimon is asking.

He sits back down. His argument leaves the men quietly thinking. No one can offer a rebuttal. Heads are nodding.

Yaakov's Proposal

Yaakov returns the floor to Shaul and Bar-Naba. They continue with their testimony. They tell the stories of the places they have been and the people they have met. There was the adventure with the sorcerer in Paphos. The crippled man in Lystra. The priests of Zeus who tried to sacrifice to them. There was Pisidian Antioch, Iconium, Attalia and of course Antioch itself. God's spirit had worked amazing wonders in every city that they had visited. There were miracles and more to tell about. Everywhere they went, Gentiles were receiving the Gospel, and they were receiving it by faith.

With their stories finally told, Yaakov takes the floor himself. All eyes are upon him. He is going to introduce an opinion, which the council will have to vote to approve or disapprove. "Brothers, listen to me," he begins warmly and with a broad sweeping gesture. "Shimon has described to us how God at first showed His concern by taking from the Gentiles a people for Himself. The words of the prophets are in agreement with this, as it is written: 'After this I will return and rebuild David's fallen tent. Its ruins I will rebuild, and I will restore it, that the remnant of men may seek the LORD, and all the Gentiles who bear my Name, says the LORD, who does these things that have been known for ages.'

"It is my judgment, therefore, that we should not make it difficult for the Gentiles who are turning to God."

What does he mean by "we should not make it difficult for the Gentiles?" The meaning is clear enough. We should not require circumcision and conversion to Judaism as the criteria for salvation. We should not require Torah (written or oral) as a criterion for salvation. Salvation is by faith.

How is this possible? Is nothing required of the Gentile believers then? Are they just to add faith in Yeshua to their paganism and carry on as if they had never heard the Gospel?

No, of course not. James continues to explain, "Instead we should write to the Gentile believers, telling them to abstain from food polluted by idols, from sexual immorality, from the meat of strangled animals and from blood. For Moses has been preached in every city from the earliest times and is read in the synagogues on every Sabbath."

The Four Minimum Requirements

James introduces four minimum laws for Gentile believers. Are these four laws a blanket exemption from the rest of Torah? Are these the only four prohibitions that apply to Gentiles? Surely not! Conspicuously absent are some major commandments, such as honoring one's father and mother, and the prohibition against murder!

Rather, the four laws James selects are socially obvious ones that will enable the Gentile converts to move among Jews. They are to abstain from meat sacrificed to idols, from meats that are not slaughtered in a kosher manner, from the consumption of blood and from sexual immorality. These four laws are not presented as if they are a replacement for the Torah, nor are they meant as the four minimum commandments that will merit salvation. They seem to be intended as a basic set of rules that will enable Jews and Gentiles to congregate together. Each law targets a specific facet of Hellenistic paganism: blood rituals; meats sacrificed to idols; ritual feasts; sexual immorality (whether overt temple prostitution or covert promiscuity).

Each of these prohibitions applies specifically to the religious practices of the pagan worship systems of the Diaspora. These four laws will ensure that the Gentiles are no longer participating in the idolatry of their local temples, thereby making it possible for them to fellowship in the synagogue.[2]

Thus, according to James' proposal, it would not be necessary for a new Gentile believer to understand and fulfill all the complex laws and traditional prohibitions of Shabbat before being reckoned part of a congregation of believers. But such a Gentile would need to make certain immediate changes in order to be received by that same congregation. Under James' proposal, the Gentile believer would not need to have his foreskin removed in order to be considered a brother in Messiah. However, he would have to give up consorting with Diana's temple prostitutes before the hand of fellowship would be extended to him.

The Rest of the Torah

As for the rest of the laws of the written Torah, Yaakov neither binds their observance upon the Gentile believers, nor does he exempt the believers from them. Instead he says, "Moses has been preached in every city from the earliest times and is read in the synagogues on every Sabbath." What does he mean by that?

Christian commentators usually suggest that James' statement about Moses being read and preached in the synagogue every week is meant only to assuage the Pharisees present. "After all," says James with a wink at the Pharisees, "Moses is taught in the synagogue every week. Therefore Torah doesn't have any real bearing on the Gentile believers." But that's absurd. How could Yaakov's words pacify the Pharisaic party if they were meant to be a dismissal of their very argument? Instead, his words seem to buttress their contention: "Torah is being taught in every city. There is no excuse not to learn it and do it!" So what does he mean?

His words mean exactly what they say. The Torah is read in the synagogue every week. At this early time in the development of the Messianic faith, the believers were still assembling within the synagogues and meeting in homes. Not until Paul moves his House of Study out of the Corinth synagogue, and into the next door house of the Gentile Titius Justus, do we see a clear change of venue where believers assemble outside of the local synagogue—and that doesn't happen until Acts chapter 18. At the time of the Jerusalem council, Jewish and Gentile believers were still assembling in the local synagogue every Shabbat.[3] And in those synagogues, the Torah was read every week.

So regarding the question of Gentile believers and their obligations toward the written Torah, James says, "The Torah is read and preached in the assembly every week." That is to say that the Gentile believers will hear the Torah. They will hear it every week. They will hear it preached every week. The obvious expectation is that hearing it read and hearing it preached will eventually lead to doing it. Given time to hear and study, the Gentile believers will eventually learn the ways of observance. But to require observance of them prior to their salvation and their participation in the Kingdom, is putting the cart before the horse.

One might paraphrase his words as, "Let's not make things difficult for these new believers. Have them do a couple of basic things so they don't get tossed out of the fellowship, but as for the rest of the Torah, they will be hearing it every week."

Are Gentile believers required to keep the Torah to earn salvation? No.

Are Gentile believers required to keep Torah at all? Of course.

As a proof text for the legitimacy of his proposal, James cites a passage from Amos.

The Proof Text

The Amos passage James quotes to support his decision is important to consider. What does that particular prophecy mean, and why does James believe it justifies the decision to allow Gentiles into the Kingdom of Heaven? Studying the passage is complicated by the fact that Acts quotes the Septuagint version of the passage. There is a significant variation between the Greek LXX (Septuagint) reading and the Hebrew reading of Amos 9:12. We had best consider both versions of the text.

The New International Version translates the Hebrew of Amos 9:11–12 as follows:

"'In that day I will restore David's fallen tent. I will repair its broken places, restore its ruins, and build it as it used to be, so that they may possess the remnant of Edom and all the nations that bear my Name,' declares the LORD, who will do these things."

The word the NIV translates as "tent" is the Hebrew word *sukkah*, which means booth or hut. Look at the condition of David's *sukkah*. It is toppled. It has broken places and ruins. It is not what it used to be, but one day it will be set back up and repaired. What does it refer to? What is David's fallen *sukkah*?

The metaphor is in no way obscure. David's fallen *sukkah* is the dynastic rule of the House of David. It is the Davidic monarchy itself.

Even in the days of Amos, the Davidic monarchy wasn't what it used to be. David's house, his *sukkah*, used to rule over a united Israel. All twelve tribes served under David, and under David's son, Solomon. There was peace and prosperity when all the tribes of Israel were unified under the shelter of David's *sukkah*. But Amos lived in a time when ten of the twelve tribes were now outside of the Davidic monarchy. They had their own king, Jeroboam II. They had their own capital and their own holy places. The Davidic monarchy, which used to rule over all the tribes of Israel, retained only two tribes: Judah and Benjamin. By comparison to what it once was, it had collapsed.

Undoubtedly the prophet saw that one day David's house would collapse completely and there would be no king from the line of David sitting on the throne of Israel or Judah. But after that, Amos tells us, David's fallen *sukkah* will be rebuilt. The dynasty will be restored. A new king, a Davidic king, will sit on the throne of all Israel again. The broken places of the monarchy will be repaired; the ruins of David's dynasty will be restored. The Kingdom of the House of David will be rebuilt as it used to be.

When that happens, the house of David will possess the "remnant of Edom and all the nations that bear the LORD's Name." It is a picture of the prophetic ideal. Things will return to the way they were in the good old days. It will be like it was in the days of Solomon, when Edom was a vassal state of Israel and all the nations brought tribute to King Solomon in Jerusalem. A Davidic king will rule out of Jerusalem. His house will possess Edom and all the nations will be subject to Him, and all the nations subject to Him will bear the LORD's Name.

What does it mean by "all the nations that bear my Name"? The Gentile nations who bear God's Name are genuine Gentile nations. They are the nations the prophet invokes in verse 7 of this same chapter. In that verse, He says, "Are not you Israelites the same to me as the Cushites? Did I not bring Israel up from Egypt, the Philistines from Caphtor and the Arameans from Kir?" God's point is that He is working with other nations too. He is not just the God of Israel; He is the God of the whole world. His plan of redemption is universal in scope and not limited only to Israel. In that day, the day when David's fallen *sukkah* is restored, all these nations that He has patiently worked with will bear God's Name and be the possession of the House of David. They will be ruled by the King of Israel, as part of the commonwealth of Israel.

The Septuagint reading of Amos 9:12 is slightly different. According to the book of Acts, James quotes a reading of the Hebrew closer to the Septuagint's rendering of the passage. That version of the passage tells us that David's fallen *sukkah* will be restored so "...that the remnant of men, and all the Gentiles upon whom my Name is called, may earnestly seek me." Therefore, the purpose of a restored Davidic king is so that all mankind can seek God.

This Septuagint version apparently read the Hebrew *Edom* as *adam*, meaning all mankind. The two variants are not contradictory; rather, they complement one another's meanings. According to the traditional Hebrew reading, the restored Davidic dynasty will possess the remnant of Edom (a Gentile nation) and, in fact, all the nations that bear God's Name. According to the LXX reading, the Davidic dynasty will be restored so that the aforementioned nations may seek the LORD.

In either case, the Gentiles who bear God's Name are Gentile nations who will be subject to an Israelite monarchy, a monarchy that will afford them the opportunity to seek the LORD.

The Proof is in the Prophets

How does this passage legitimize the decision of Yaakov and the Jerusalem Council? In what way does this passage justify a Gentile exemption from immediate circumcision and full conversion to Judaism?

The key to understanding how Yaakov uses the passage is identifying the Davidic king. To Yaakov and the believers in Jerusalem, David's restored *sukkah* is Yeshua.[4] He is the Davidic king who has come to rebuild the monarchy of Israel. Yeshua is the repairer of the broken places, the restorer of the ruins, who rebuilds the legitimate throne of Israel. According to the Amos passage, the restored Davidic king will include those Gentiles who bear God's Name.

The Gentiles whom Paul and Bar-Naba are encountering fit the prophet's description. They are Gentiles from the nations who identify themselves with God's Name and seek after God because of the kingship of Yeshua. However, if all Gentiles who seek the LORD through Yeshua must convert to Judaism under Pharisaic auspices, they cease to be reckoned as Gentiles at all. According to the Pharisaic perspective, Gentiles who undergo circumcision and conventional conversion can only be reckoned as Jews. But by virtue of the fact that Amos calls them Gentiles who bear God's Name and seek the LORD, they cannot be Jews! The moment that they are circumcised, they would become Jews and no longer be Gentiles who bear God's Name and seek the LORD. But the prophecy, which is future tense, clearly speaks of these God seekers as Gentiles. Therefore, in the days of Messiah, there will be both Jews and Gentiles—an impossibility if all Gentiles are forced to be circumcised as part of a rabbinically formulated conversion to Judaism. How could Jews be called Gentiles?

Amos's Gentiles are vassals of the Israelite king. As such, they are part of the commonwealth of Israel, with full rights as citizens of Israel. They are bound to the laws of the king of Israel. However, they are not blood Israelites. They are by blood, "Edomites, Cushites, Philistines, Arameans" and peoples of every tribe, tongue and nation on earth. They are Gentiles, bearing God's Name, seeking the LORD and serving the restored Davidic Dynasty, even Yeshua the King. Thus, they have a legitimate place in the kingdom, but they still maintain their own ethnic identity. They are part of the kingdom of Israel even though they are Edomites, Cushites, Philistines, Arameans. They are vassals of the king of the Jews, but they are not Jews.

Isaiah picks up this theme of Gentiles seeking the LORD and being called by the Name of the LORD. Regarding this inclusion of

Gentiles he writes, "One will say, 'I belong to the LORD'; another will call himself by the name of Jacob; still another will write on his hand, 'The LORD's,' and will take the name Israel."[5] The Isaiah passage is similar to the Amos proof text because it includes Gentiles who have chosen to identify themselves with the name of Israel and the Name of the God of Israel. Isaiah refers to this idealized Israel as the authentic *Yeshurun. Yeshurun* is a name for Israel that occurs only four times in the Hebrew Scriptures—the other three occasions are all in Deuteronomy. It means "upright one," and is a term of endearment for Israel.

Isaiah's descriptions of *Yeshurun* speak of the ideal Israel: a forgiven and redeemed nation walking in upright obedience to the covenants, satiated with God's Spirit and incorporating people from all nations.

> Do not be afraid, O Jacob, my servant, Yeshurun, whom I have chosen. For I will pour water on the thirsty land, and streams on the dry ground; I will pour out my Spirit on your offspring, and my blessing on your descendants. They will spring up like grass in a meadow, like poplar trees by flowing streams. One will say, "I belong to the LORD"; another will call himself by the name of Jacob; still another will write on his hand, "The LORD's," and will take the name Israel.
> (Isaiah 44:2–5)

ENDNOTES

1 This is a cogent point because the entire conversion ritual into Judaism is a contrivance of the Oral Law and rabbinic tradition. See Hegg (2003) *It is Often Said,* Volume 1: "Torah is a Burden" for a clear exposition on the passage and the decision of the Jerusalem Council.

2 Again, see Hegg (2003) *It is Often Said,* Volume 1: "Torah is a Burden" for a clear explanation of the four minimum commandments and how they related to idolatry.

3 In fact, the formulation of the 19th benediction (a curse against believers) by the council at Yavneh around 95 CE implies that believers were still in the synagogues at the close of the 1st century.

4 According to Sanhedrin 96b–97a, David's restored tent is identified as Messiah.

5 Isaiah 44:4

Gentile Israel

10
Gentile Israel
Galatians

Apparently not everyone agreed with the decision of the Jerusalem council.

Consider, for example, the situation in Galatia. The Galatians were new believers, converts out of paganism. They were the Gentiles of the city of Pisidian-Antioch, Iconium and Derbe. Faith in Yeshua was their only rite of conversion. But subsequent to their conversion out of the kingdom of darkness and into the Kingdom of God, some brothers and sisters from Jerusalem paid them a visit. These visitors were Jewish brothers and sisters who still held fast to the conviction that only Israelites could have a place in God's covenant. Only Israel could be saved. Only Israel was in the Kingdom.

The visitors from Jerusalem taught that it was necessary, in addition to faith in Yeshua, that the Galatian Gentiles should also be circumcised—thereby signifying their formal conversion to Judaism. According to these fellows, only after circumcision could the Gentiles be regarded as truly a part of the Kingdom. Faith in Messiah alone was not adequate. According to these visitors, the Galatians also needed to become Israelites.

Paul responded to this teaching with his scathing letter to the Galatians. Regarding those brothers, he lost his temper and accused them of teaching, "some other gospel." He said, "Let them be eternally condemned!" He even took it a step further than that. He said, "As for those agitators, I wish they would go the whole way and emasculate themselves!"[1] Consider what the Apostle is saying. As if eternal damnation was not bad enough, Paul wanted them to be eternally damned with less than their whole apparatus!

Paul's rancor reveals his priorities. The Gospel of Salvation, full and free, specifically salvation proclaimed to the Gentiles, salvation by faith through grace alone, was the very heartbeat of passion that fueled that old Pharisee's life. The Gentile inclusion through faith in Yeshua was the Gospel to Paul! That was the good news. To him, anything that obscured that simple truth was some other gospel.

The Apostle to the Uncircumcised

Subsequent to the Jerusalem council of Acts 15, Paul referred to himself as the official "apostle to the Gentiles." In Romans 11:13, for example, he identified himself as "the apostle to the Gentiles." The Greek word he uses for Gentiles is *ethnos*, from which we derive the word "ethnicity." Paul identified himself as the apostle to the ethnic nationalities. His description of his apostleship is contrasted against Peter's apostleship to the Jews. Carefully read Paul's words in Galatians 2:7, 8.

> They saw that I had been entrusted with the task of preaching the gospel to the uncircumcised, just as Peter had been to the circumcised. For God, who was at work in the ministry of Peter as an apostle to the circumcised, was also at work in my ministry as an apostle to the Gentiles.

In this passage, Paul uses the term uncircumcised (*akrobustia*) synonymously with the term Gentiles (*ethnos*). From Paul's perspective, to be uncircumcised was to be a Gentile: one from the Nations. No double meanings are implied here. Paul's world is very black and white. *Ethnos* is *ethnos*; Gentiles are Gentiles.

The Greek word *akrobustia*, which we are translating as uncircumcised, is perhaps more honestly rendered as foreskinned. It is a contraction of two Greek words. *Akron* means tip or extremity. *Posthe* means "the masculine member." The *akrobustia* is the extremity of that masculine member's tip, that is, the foreskin. The gentlemen Paul referred to as *akrobustia* would have been men still in possession of such.

As evidenced from Galatians 2:7, 8, the foreskinned people are non-Israelites: *ethnos*. Peter, on the other hand, is the apostle to the *peritome*, that is the circumcised.

But wait. Suppose you didn't have a foreskin. Take Paul's convert Lydia, for example: a weaver of purple cloth and, more to the point, a woman. Was she outside of Paul's purview because she was a woman and he was the apostle to the foreskinned? The point that needs to be made is the term "foreskinned" does not refer to the literal state of being circumcised or uncircumcised. It is used categorically to refer to those Gentile believers who had not made a conversion to Judaism. In a similar way, the term "circumcision" is used categorically to refer to Jews, and to proselytes who have come to Judaism via the rabbinic conversion ritual. That's why Paul is able to say, "Circumcision is nothing and uncircumcision is nothing. Keeping God's commands is what counts."[2] Notice the apparent contradiction: Circumcision is one of God's commands. If keeping God's commands is what counts, then surely circumcision is something.

The way Paul uses the terminology, circumcision refers specifically to the rabbinic conversion ritual, not to the written Torah command of circumcision. Thus Paul is saying, "Converting to Judaism or not is meaningless. Keeping God's commands is what counts."

Paul, then, is the apostle to the "foreskinned," by which he means Gentiles.

Peter is the apostle to the "circumcised," by which Paul means Jews and proselytes to Judaism.

If a foreskinned person (*akrobustia*) should choose to follow the rabbinic conversion ritual, which includes circumcision (*peritome*), he is no longer regarded as a Gentile (*ethnos*). Indeed, such a person has become an Israelite, specifically Jewish. In contrast, Paul, the apostle to the foreskinned (*akrobustia*), is zealous to defend their right to retain their foreskins. If they were compelled to be circumcised before being admitted to the Kingdom, that would have been the equivalent of declaring that Messiah's atonement was insufficient to save men with foreskins! If they were compelled to undergo a conversion to Judaism, the implication would be that Messiah was unable to save Gentiles.

Paul Responds

So Paul responded to the Galatians by saying, "Are you so foolish? After beginning with the Spirit, are you now trying to attain your goal by human effort?"[3] The specific human effort Paul was speaking of was a formal conversion to Judaism through the rite of circumcision. In the eyes of men, circumcision allowed for a conventional, physical, human position in Israel. It was a position attained through natural, physical, human methods. Paul asked the Galatians, "Are you now trying to attain your goal by human effort? By natural means? Are you trying to buy your way into the Kingdom by converting to Judaism?"

Paul's letter to the Galatians is a fierce, impassioned argument against the requirement of Gentile conversion through rabbinic Judaism. Paul contended that it was not necessary for Gentiles to convert to Judaism in order to be a legitimate part of the People of God. It was not necessary for them to be reckoned as part of the physical Seed of Abraham because the promise of the covenant of the Seed of Abraham had already received its ultimate fulfillment in the one singular seed: namely Yeshua.

In Galatians 3:16 he wrote, "The promises [given to Abraham] were spoken to Abraham and to his seed. The Scripture does not say 'and to seeds,' meaning many people, but 'and to your seed,' meaning one person, who is Messiah." This means that the receipt of the promises given to Abraham is not based upon an individual being part of the physical seed of Abraham. After all, Paul argues, the promise was not given to "seeds." "Seeds" in the plural form would suggest the many physical descendents of Abraham, the Israelite lineage. Rather, he says, it was given to a singular "seed." The singular "seed" of Abraham is Messiah. Thus, according to Paul, Messiah is the Seed of Abraham. Messiah is the promised seed and the fulfillment of the seed promises of the Scripture. Because of that, when Gentiles (those not of Abraham's seed) place faith in Messiah, the Seed of Abraham, they are spiritually connected to that seed.

When Gentiles place their faith in the Seed of Abraham (Yeshua), then all the passages and prophecies which speak of Abraham's Seed blessing all nations, and the Seed of Israel becoming a community of nations, and the Seed of Ephraim and Manasseh becoming a fullness of nations, all of these prophecies are ultimately fulfilled in the Seed that is Messiah. From Paul's vantage, for a Gentile believer to become circumcised under the auspices of a rabbinic conversion to Judaism was redundant. It was, if anything, an affront to Messiah because it implied that faith in Messiah was not adequate to secure a position in the covenant with Israel. It was a denial of the Gospel. Paul says,

"If you allow yourselves to be circumcised (that is to undergo a formal conversion into Judaism as a necessary component of your salvation), Messiah is of no value to you."[4] Messiah is of no value because the convert has opted to accomplish his participation in Israel through his own physical efforts. To Paul's way of thinking, ritual conversion after salvation is like campaigning for an office for which you have already been elected.

Paul responded to the bid for Gentile conversion to Judaism by forbidding the Galatians to circumcise. He may have even gone so far as to discourage all Gentile believers from circumcision as long as the commandment of circumcision was being misunderstood.[5] In the case of Gentiles with authentic Israelite heritage, however, he does not hesitate to circumcise. In fact, Paul personally oversaw Timothy's circumcision. Gentiles without Israelite bloodlines, like Titus[6] or the Galatians, he encourages to remain uncircumcised, at least as long as circumcision is understood as the ticket into the Kingdom. Gentiles with Israelite blood, like Timothy, he circumcises without hesitation.

Misreading Paul

Paul goes on to develop this argument from several angles. Later readers of the epistle, who were not aware of the contextual situation, interpreted Galatians to be an anti-Torah and anti-Jewish work. Based upon this sad and deeply flawed misreading of Galatians, we Christians jettisoned most of Torah observance and our connections to Judaism. We began to believe that anyone who attempted to keep a commandment of Torah was under the curse of the Torah. In retrospect, it was an absurd proposition, but to those who expounded the idea, it was consistent with their misreading of Galatians.

But Paul was not preaching against Gentiles keeping the Torah. He wasn't even preaching against Gentiles becoming circumcised. He was preaching against Gentiles undergoing the conventional conversion into Judaism in order to achieve salvation.

It would appear that the epistle to the Galatians was already being misunderstood even in Paul's own lifetime. When he arrives at Jerusalem in Acts 21, James warns him that there are false rumors going around to the effect that Paul is teaching "the Jews who live among the Gentiles to turn away from Moses, telling them not to circumcise their children."[7] Acts 21 makes clear that the rumors were indeed false rumors, but it shows us how Paul's arguments concerning circumcision were already being misunderstood and misused. Then there is Peter's famous comment regarding the interpretation of Paul's epistles. In 2 Peter he writes, "Paul's letters contain some things that are hard to understand, which ignorant and unstable people distort, as they do the other Scriptures, to their own destruction."

If sorting out Paul's arguments was difficult for the first century believers, how much more so for later generations? One can hardly wonder that we would have misunderstood.

Ironically, the epistle to the Galatians is the very scripture that Christians most often use to refute Gentile believers who are beginning to return to their Jewish roots. As Christians begin to involve themselves in the various aspects of their heritage (such as Sabbath observance, kosher laws, daily prayer, etc.), they are often rebuked by other believers quoting from Galatians.

But that is turning it exactly backwards! Galatians was written to argue for Gentile inclusion in Israel, not Gentile exclusion from Israel!

Abraham our Father

As Paul fights for the legitimacy of Gentile inclusion in Israel, one of the angles of argument he develops is the believer's connection to the Patriarchs. He builds a premise that says all who have placed faith in Messiah are spiritual sons and daughters of Abraham. Years later, Paul reworked that thesis in the fourth chapter of his epistle to the Romans. In eloquent and measured terms, he clearly states that just as Abraham was credited with righteousness before he was circumcised, so too the Gentile believers are credited with righteousness apart from any Jewish conversion ritual. Therefore, Abraham is the "father of all who believe" so that the "promise may be guaranteed to all Abraham's seed—not only to those who are legally the seed of Abraham (i.e. blood Israelites and converts to Judaism), but also to those who are of the faith of Abraham. He is the father of all."[8]

Almost 1,000 years later, Moses Maimonides found himself fighting the same kinds of battles Paul of Tarsus once fought in Galatians and Romans. In his day, a dispute had arisen among the

Jewish communities about proselytes. Could a proselyte pray the Amidah? Could a former Gentile really say the words, "Blessed are you LORD our God, God of our Fathers, God of Abraham, God of Isaac, God of Jacob"? Some felt that such a prayer should be reserved only for the legitimate heirs of the Patriarchs, and that it was somehow not right for converts to Judaism to say those words.

Maimonides responded by saying, "Anyone who becomes a convert throughout the generations and anyone who unifies the Name of the Holy One as it is written in the Torah is a disciple of our father Abraham, and all of them are members of his household… hence you may say: 'Our God and God of our fathers,' for Abraham, peace be upon him, is your father… Because you have come beneath the wings of the Divine Presence and attached yourself to God, there is no difference between us and you… You certainly may recite the blessings, 'Who has chosen us,' 'Who has given us,' 'Who has caused us to inherit' and 'Who has separated us,' for the Creator has already chosen you and has separated you from the nations and has given you the Torah." [9]

Maimonides meant to assure Gentile converts to Judaism that they had every right to pray those words, "God of our fathers, God of Abraham, God of Isaac and God of Jacob." His conclusion was not far removed from Paul's own. As disciples of our father Abraham, following after the faith of Abraham, we Gentile believers have the privilege to say "Avraham Avinu," "Abraham our Father." For there is neither Jew nor Gentile, slave nor free, male nor female, for we are all one in Messiah Yeshua.[10]

Gentile Israel

An even greater irony is that while the Jewish people are so often hated, reviled, and persecuted, there are so many groups of people trying to claim that they are Israelites. The Mormons teach that Native Americans are descended from Israelites who left Jerusalem for the New World before their city was destroyed by the Babylonians. Others say the Israelite tribes fathered the Asians or the black races.

Historically, Christianity has taught Replacement Theology—the belief that God divorced Israel and married the Church. Gentile Christians then become the New Israel, the New People of God, while the Jews are left pathetic and unwanted outside of God's covenant. In this traditional Christian worldview, we Gentile Christians become the inheritors of the promises of God while the Jews inherit only eternal punishment!

Christianity was not the first religion to introduce Replacement Theology. The Samaritans had a head start on us by almost 700 years. Samaritans are actual descendents of the Ten Northern Tribes. When the Northern tribes were deported, and foreign populations were imported by Assyria, the resulting conglomeration of bloodlines and religions became the Samaritans. They were not quite Israelites, but not quite Gentiles either. They wrongly came to believe that they were the real and true Israel. Coincidently, they called themselves the "House of Joseph." Josephus writes about them as follows, but his description could be applied to countless other sects and religions that have come and gone as well:

> And when they see the Jews in prosperity, they pretend that they are changed, and allied to them, and call them kinsmen, as though they were derived from Joseph, and had by that means an original alliance with them; but when they see them falling into a low condition, they say they are no way related to them, and that the Jews have no right to expect any kindness or marks of family from them, but they declare that they are sojourners, that come from other countries. (Josephus *Antiquities* 9.14.3)

Replacement Theology was the normal theology for all branches of Christianity for most of our 2000 years of history. Only in recent years have we reexamined this fundamental presupposition of our faith and found it to be unscriptural and unwarranted. Only in recent decades have Christian thinkers and theologians emerged who have deliberately rejected Replacement Theology.

Why I am of the Seed of Abraham

The best we can determine from the historical record, is that the Galatians were originally Celtic people.[11] The Celts are also my forebears because my mother is a Kelly, an Irishwoman. As much as I might fancy being a physical descendent of Abraham, Isaac and Jacob, the fact is that I, like the Galatians, am a descendent of the Celtic peoples.

So my ancestors definitely were not Israelites. They were wild people who worshipped cruel gods, gods that demanded human sacrifices and human blood. Their priests were called "druids"—mysterious men who communed with nature and the world of the spirits. The Celtic world was a world in-between, a world on the edge of borders or across waters. My ancestors lived in fear of this shadowy world of the unknown, this world of malevolent spirits and bloodthirsty gods, of sacrifices on the equinox, of sacred stones and sacred trees. My ancestors ran naked on the battle fields, bodies painted with woad, shouting and screaming to terrify their enemies, then feasting on the blood of their victims. It's not a very pretty family portrait.

In Genesis 22:18, God promises Abraham, "In thy seed shall all the nations of the earth be blessed." Does this passage mean that Abraham's seed must be scattered through all the nations on the earth? Does it mean that all nations will be descended from Abraham's seed?

My claim to the inheritance of the Kingdom and my place of standing in Israel is not based on my genetic descent. The truth that lays claim on me is much deeper, much more profound and much more powerful than Jewish ancestry. I am part of the seed of Abraham because I am part of the body of Messiah, and Messiah is the Seed of Abraham.

When a Gentile (or an Israelite for that matter) places faith in Messiah, he becomes a part of the body of Messiah. Paul wrote, "Do you not know that your bodies are members of Messiah Himself?"[12] The Master taught us that when we place our faith in Him, we are in Him and He in us. We are no longer ourselves alone, but we are invested with a share of His identity. His vivifying life force, even His very identity, is planted within us.

In the same mystical and inexplicable sense that He is One with the Father because He is in the Father and the Father is in Him, so too we are made a part of this circle of unity when we come to faith. The Master tells us that He is in us and we are in Him. We are one with Him. As we partake of His body, we become His body.

Paul tells us that Messiah is "the seed of Abraham." Yeshua is Abraham's seed in a sense even more true and eternal than Isaac is. Yeshua is the ultimate fulfillment of those seed promises, and the promise is one of blessing for all nations in Abraham's seed. The Hebrew of Genesis 22:18 (and subsequent repetitions) specifically use the preposition "in." All nations will be blessed in Abraham's seed.

How do we enter into Abraham's seed, especially if that seed is one man? We enter into the seed of Abraham when we enter into Messiah. Only in Messiah can one be truly in Abraham's seed!

The Master told us, "I am in my Father, and you are in me, and I am in you."[13] If we are in Messiah and He is in us, then we are in the seed of Abraham and the seed of Abraham is in us.

Paul said, "Therefore, if anyone is in Messiah, he is a new creation; the old has gone, the new has come!"[14] My Gentile *ethnos* is no longer relevant as regards my place in the Kingdom. I am in Messiah. I am in the Seed of Abraham. I am a new creation. I am part of the Seed of Abraham.

If I accept those truths, then I am no longer in any need of claiming Israelite ancestry; I have no need to search for a Jew in my genealogy. If, however, my identity in Messiah is not adequate to assure my position in Israel, then I have not fully understood my new identity.

If I have not embraced the reality of Messiah in me and myself in Messiah, then I am left outside trying to understand my position in the People of God. However, if I have admitted that through faith I am in Messiah the Seed of Abraham and Messiah the Seed of Abraham is in me, I need no further identification. To look for something more, something physical, something outside of my relationship with Messiah in order to offer me a sense of identity, is essentially the very sin the Galatians were committing.

Paul concludes his argument by saying, "Neither circumcision nor uncircumcision means anything; what counts is a new creation. Peace and mercy to all who follow this rule, even to the Israel of God."[15]

When he says "circumcision" he means being a natural Israelite, specifically a Jew, whether by birth or by auspices of rabbinic conversion.

When he says "uncircumcision," he means being a natural Gentile, specifically one who has not made a formal conversion to Judaism.

When he says "new creation," he means Israelites or Gentiles who belong to Messiah.

When he says Israel of God, he means all of us.

ENDNOTES

1 Galatians 5:12

2 1 Corinthians 7:19

3 Galatians 3:3

4 Galatians 5:2

5 1 Corinthians 7:18

6 Galatians 2:3

7 Acts 21:21

8 Romans 4:16

9 Kling, 1987, pg. 4

10 Galatians 3:28

11 I once read a fanciful theory proposing that the region of Galatia takes its name from the Hebrew word for "exile," which is *Galut*. Thus, the book of *Galut*-ians has this Hebrew root word embedded within it. According to this theory, Israelites taken into exile by Assyria in 721 BCE became the early inhabitants of Galatia. Still in possession of some Hebrew phonology, they named their new land "Exile." The author of this theory supposed that Paul was in Galatia seeking out these lost Israelites. Thus, the Gentiles of Galatia would have been long lost descendents of the Ten Tribes.

In contrast to that fanciful theory, the Galatians were actually a Celtic people that migrated down from Europe around 300 BC. At the time of the Israelite exile, when the Ten Tribes were "lost," the Celts were already settling the region of Galatia. So their history predates the Israelite diaspora, and they could not have been part of the Ten Tribes.

What's more, Paul speaks of the Galatians in a provincial sense rather than an ethnic sense. Most scholars agree that the Galatians to whom he addressed his epistles were the various ethnic groups of Pisidian-Antioch, Iconium, Lystra and Derbe. These included Phrygians and Lycaonians.

12 1 Corinthians 6:15

13 John 14:20

14 2 Corinthians 5:17

15 Galatians 6:15–16

The Eternal Purpose of God

11
The Eternal Purpose of God
Ephesians

Far away, across many seas, down ancient roads and over steep hills is the place of God, the joy of the whole earth, the city of the Great King, Jerusalem. How many hands have been stretched out in prayer toward her walls? How many feet have walked the pilgrim miles to her gates? "I rejoiced with those who said to me, 'Let us go to the House of the LORD.' Our feet are standing in your gates, O Jerusalem."[1]

For in the days of the apostles the Temple of God was still there. Imagine the joy. Imagine the anticipation of the pilgrimage. Imagine our first sight of the Temple, our entrance through the city gates, our climb toward the Temple Mount. Immersed and purified, we are prepared to worship. Step by step, we climb the monumental stairway. It is a festival day. It is a time appointed to meet with the LORD. Our voices are joined with the voices of the other worshippers. We pass through the great gates and enter the Court of the Gentiles. The House of God is before us now. We can see the smoke of the altar rising over the Beautiful Gate. We can catch the scent of the incense on the air. We can hear the song of the Levites. Our hearts are pounding within us. Since we first heard of Him, we have longed for this moment. We mean to enter the House of God. We have come, we are here, we are with God's people and we are entering His House.

Then there is a wall... a partition made of stone, three cubits high. Spaced at equal intervals along the wall are pillars bearing inscriptions, some in Greek letters, and some in Roman letters. These signs say that no foreigner should go within the sanctuary;[2] that trespassers enter on the pain of death.[3]

We non-Jews may go no further. We sons and daughters of the nations may look on the House of God, longing for the intimacy of His table, but we are on this side of the wall. His House, His People, even the blood atonement of His sacrifice are all on the other side of the wall. The inescapable conclusion is that we are on the outside.

It was this very wall the Apostle Paul was walking past when he was accosted by an angry mob. They were not angry with him for teaching the death and resurrection of Messiah; they were angry with him for teaching Gentile inclusion in Israel. They were angry with him for filling the synagogue with Gentiles and declaring that those Gentiles were "joint heirs with Israel." How dare he disregard the dividing wall?

Not that he had actually brought Gentiles into the inner courts of the Temple. Worse than that, he had transgressed the metaphoric wall separating Israel from non-Israel. He had obscured the sharp lines of who was in and who was out. His disregard for the metaphoric wall between Jew and Gentile led to his arrest, imprisonment and eventual trial in Rome. You may recall that in chapter one, we left Paul in Rome musing over the mystery of the Gospel. Remember that to Paul, the mystery of the Gospel was not the mysterious incarnation, death and resurrection of Yeshua. The mystery was that the Gentiles had somehow been included in Israel. Somehow, the dividing wall had been broken down.

It is time to seriously weigh the words of Ephesians 2 and 3 and see if we might be able to unravel some of the mystery of Messiah.

Breaking Down the Wall

In the last chapter, I confessed my own Celtic ancestry. I admitted that my forebears were not ancient Israelites. My earliest grandfather Kelly was a pagan Gentile through and through. We can be fairly certain that he didn't have a drop of Abraham's DNA in his body, and even if he did, it afforded him precious little good. He was a complete stranger to the House of Israel, a foreigner to the covenant promises and without knowledge of God. Nonetheless, it is this fact, that my ancestors were godless strangers to the covenants of Israel, that they were far from God, and even in the possession of the demonic powers and principalities of this fallen world, it is precisely this which inspires Paul. It is this very fact that Paul finds so compelling about me and other Gentiles.

> For it is by grace you have been saved, through faith—and this not from yourselves, it is the gift of God—not by works, so that no one can boast. For we are God's workmanship, created in Christ Jesus to do good works, which God prepared in advance for us to do. Therefore, remember that formerly you who are Gentiles by birth and called "uncircumcised" by those who call themselves "the circumcision" (that done in the body by the hands of men)—remember that at that time you were separate from Messiah, excluded from citizenship in Israel and foreigners to the covenants of the promise, without hope and without God in the world. But now in Messiah Yeshua you who once were far away have been brought near through the blood of Messiah. (Ephesians 2:8–13)

Paul is very clear about our identity as Gentiles. He makes it explicitly obvious that we were excluded from Israel. As unredeemed Gentiles, we were foreigners to the covenants of Israel. We were without even a claim to the covenants of the forefathers. According to Paul, we had no share in Israel, no rights to the promises of the covenants. None. No claim to an inheritance in Jacob.

Subsequent to our salvation, however, there has been a change in our status. Paul says that, while we were formerly Gentiles, somehow, through some mystery, our identity has changed. "But now in Messiah Yeshua you who once were far away have been brought near through the blood of Messiah." We who were once far away have been brought near. We have been brought into Israel. A radical transformation has occurred.

This transformation is in many ways equivalent to the legal transformation that occurs when a Gentile passes through the rabbinically prescribed ritual of becoming a proselyte. However, it is not that conversion ritual which Paul is speaking about in Ephesians. Here he is making the point that the Gentile believers have received this new identity without a formal ritual conversion. "Not by works lest any man boast," he says, and by works he means the conventional rabbinic conversion ritual, complete with the works of circumcision, immersion and sacrifice. Those are the "works" of the Pauline Epistles.

The conversion Paul is speaking of is "not by works, but by grace through faith." It is the grace of God bestowed simply and purely through faith in Yeshua. He goes on to explain the mechanics of this process in verse 2:14. "For He [Yeshua] Himself is our peace, who has made the two one and has destroyed the barrier, the dividing wall of hostility."

The image of a dividing wall of hostility between Jew and Gentile is borrowed directly from the architecture of the Jerusalem Temple. Paul invokes the image of that wall of separation between the Court of the Gentiles and the Court of Israel. That wall of separation, which forbade Gentiles on pain of death from entering the Court of Israel and the Temple of God, is a potent metaphor for the theological exclusion of Gentiles from Israel. According to Paul, the wall of separation, the barrier between the people of the nations and the people of God, is destroyed by Messiah.

Abolishing the Torah

As we study through Ephesians 2, it's worth taking a careful look at how the New International Version expresses some of these ideas. From our standpoint, the NIV takes a curious turn. The central clause of verses 14 and 15 reads as follows:

"For he himself is our peace, who has made the two one and has destroyed the barrier, the dividing wall of hostility, by abolishing in his flesh the law with its commandments and regulations." (Ephesians 2:14–15)

The translators of the NIV, like most translators of English versions of the Bible, have rendered the Greek to say that not only did Messiah's death bring peace between Jew and Gentile, but it also abolished the Torah. How convenient for us Gentiles! Not only do we receive full rights of participation and citizenship in Israel, but we are scot-free from acting like it at all. In one quick action, Messiah supposedly erased the distinction between Jews and Gentiles, and also erased the whole Torah of Moses. Never mind that business about "Do not think I have come to abolish the law," we have the evidence right here in Ephesians! The Torah, with its commandments and regulations, has been abolished!

Such a passage would certainly seem to eliminate the need for Gentiles (or Jews for that matter) to observe any of the Mosaic covenant. Since Messiah has abolished the law with its commandments and regulations, it would be superfluous for anyone to keep Sabbath, to keep kosher or even to refrain from covetousness, adultery or idolatry. Jew and Gentile are thus made alike on the basis that they seemingly have no obligations of identity of any kind.

The actual sense of Ephesians 2:14, 15 is not that Messiah's flesh abolishes the Torah, it is the enmity being abolished. For clarity, it should read, "For He Himself is our peace, who has made the two one and has destroyed the barrier, the dividing wall, by abolishing in His flesh the enmity..."[4] It is the enmity between Jew and Gentile that Messiah's flesh abolished, not the Torah. Specification of the source of this enmity follows immediately. "The Torah with its commandments and regulations." It is the Torah's commandments and regulations which have caused the enmity between Jew and Gentile.

How does the Torah cause enmity between Jew and Gentile? We have already seen how the Oral Law, the rabbinic interpretation of Torah, excluded Gentiles.[5] The Greek word for "regulations" speaks specifically to those man-made contrivances, not to the actual Torah. According to those oral commandments and regulations, one needed to make a formal conversion to Judaism before participating in Israel. The dividing wall of the Temple is itself an architectural innovation based on rabbinic interpretation. In first century Jerusalem, the dividing wall of hostility was more than just a metaphor.

But the written Torah actually sets up parameters for participation in Israel, such as circumcision, Sabbath observance, and abstaining from adultery. Those are all commandments and ordinances found in the Torah. Observance of the commandments and ordinances is compulsory for Israelites because the Torah is Israel's covenant with God. The Gentiles, however, as strangers to the covenants of promise, are oblivious to these laws. The result is a sharp distinction between Jew and Gentile. Add to that the first century theological supposition that Torah was only for Jews, and it created a very distinct and clear line of separation between Jew and Gentile.

There is enmity engendered by the Torah between Israelite and Gentile, and the enmity is this: Israel is God's chosen and redeemed people, and the Gentiles are not. Israel is in covenant with the Father and the Gentiles are not. Every command and ordinance given to Israel marked out the parameters of who Israel was and who Israel was not. The Torah determined who was in and who was out.

The enmity that Messiah abolished is this separation between Jew and Gentile. It is abolished in the sense that Messiah has brought Gentile believers into Israel. He seats them at the table with Israel and invites them to be partakers in the New Covenant with Israel. As Gentiles brought into covenant through Messiah begin to engage in the commandments and ordinances along with Israel, the line of distinction, the dividing wall of hostility vanishes. The enmity between Jewish and Gentile believers, caused by commandments and ordinances, is abolished in Messiah's flesh. How so? Because Messiah brings the Gentiles into the fold of Israel.

The prophet Isaiah provides a vivid illustration of this principal. He declares that the stranger who keeps the Sabbath and holds fast to God's covenant will be received in the innermost courts of the Temple. His sacrifices will be received on the altar, and the Temple will be a House of Prayer for Gentiles from every nation (Isaiah 56:7). It was probably this very passage that Paul had in mind as he wrote of Messiah abolishing the dividing wall. For the dividing wall, which would forbid the Gentile from entering the Temple to offer sacrifice, is completely absent in Isaiah's Messianic-age prophecy:

> And foreigners who bind themselves to the LORD to serve Him, to love the name of the LORD, and to worship Him, all who keep the Sabbath without desecrating it and who hold fast to my covenant—these I will bring to my holy mountain and give them joy in my house of prayer. Their burnt offerings and sacrifices will be accepted on my altar; for my house will be called a house of prayer for all nations. (Isaiah 56:6–7)

Therefore the Ephesians passage (2:14–15, quoted earlier from the NIV) is not a contradiction of the Master's words in Matthew 5:17 ("Do not think I have come to abolish the Torah..."), nor is it a textual justification to sin and sin boldly. Instead, it shows us how Gentiles are able to retain their Gentile identity while at the same time being regarded as part of Israel, living out the law of Israel. "For He Himself is our peace."

Because the enmity has been abolished, Gentiles need not find a genetic justification for keeping the laws and ordinances of Torah nor must they make a formal conversion to Judaism. The enmity of distinction has been removed; the laws and ordinances of Torah are open to Gentiles. The dividing wall has been removed. Gentiles are free to move from the metaphoric Court of the Gentiles into the metaphoric Court of Israel. They are given free access to the Torah life that identifies Israel; they are given access to the House of God.

One New Man

> His purpose was to create in Himself one new man out of the two, thus making peace, and in this one body to reconcile both of them to God through the cross, by which He put to death their hostility. He came and preached peace to you who were far away [Gentiles] and peace to those who were near [Israel]. For through Him we both have access to the Father by one Spirit.
>
> Consequently, you are no longer foreigners and aliens [Gentiles], but fellow citizens with God's people and members of God's household [Israel], built on the foundation of the apostles and prophets, with Messiah Yeshua Himself as the chief cornerstone.
>
> In Him [Messiah] the whole building is joined together and rises to become a holy temple in the Lord. And in Him you too are being built together to become a dwelling in which God lives by His Spirit. (Ephesians 2:15–22)

Paul is the apostle to the Gentiles, the apostle to the strangers and aliens to God's people. The good news is that through Messiah, we are strangers and aliens no more.

We who were far away have been brought near. We who had no share or claim in Israel have been granted the status of citizenship in Israel. We are citizens of Israel through Messiah. This is not just symbolic status. This is a real position in and among the People of God.

It is notable that Paul never makes an argument for Israel's inclusion in the Church. Israel is not being joined to the Church. Jews are not being made into Gentiles. Quite the opposite. Paul's theology has Gentiles entering Israel, joining with Israel as fellow citizens. We are strangers brought near. Israel by faith.

Jew and Gentile are joined together, like the two halves of Ezekiel's stick,[6] to make one new man. Paul compares this process to the bringing together of various building materials in order to make a Holy Temple for the LORD to reside in. He says, "In Him [Messiah] the whole building is joined together and rises to become a holy temple in the Lord. And in Him you too are being built together to become a dwelling in which God lives by His Spirit."

Paul means to tell us that not only has the dividing wall which once forbade us from entering the Temple been broken, but we are actually being made into a Spiritual Temple for God to reside within. Gentile believers are being built together with Jewish believers into an eternal Temple.

The Mystery of Messiah and the Eternal Purpose of God

> For this reason I, Paul, the prisoner of Messiah Yeshua for the sake of you Gentiles—Surely you have heard about the administration of God's grace that was given to me for you, that is, the mystery made known to me by revelation, as I have already written briefly.
>
> In reading this, then, you will be able to understand my insight into the mystery of Messiah, which was not made known to men in other generations as it has now been revealed by the Spirit to God's holy apostles and prophets. This mystery is that through the gospel the Gentiles are heirs together with Israel, members together of one body, and sharers together in the promise in Messiah Yeshua.

> I became a servant of this Gospel by the gift of God's grace given me through the working of His power. Although I am less than the least of all God's people, this grace was given me: to preach to the Gentiles the unsearchable riches of Messiah, and to make plain to everyone the administration of this mystery, which for ages past was kept hidden in God, who created all things.
>
> His intent was that now, through the church, the manifold wisdom of God should be made known to the rulers and authorities in the heavenly realms, according to His Eternal Purpose which He accomplished in Messiah Yeshua our Lord. (Ephesians 3:1–9)

What is Paul's big mystery of Messiah which for ages past was kept hidden in God? The mystery is that Gentiles are heirs together with Israel. It may be somewhat matter-of-fact for us now, but it was a shock to first century Jews, even as it remains a shock to many Jews today. It is a staggering proposition. How can Israel be open to all nations and still retain her integrity as a people set apart and holy? Isn't that a contradiction? How can Israel be the chosen people if everyone has a free ticket to be part of Israel?

It is a mystery that demands an explanation. It seems so irrational. What's the point of calling out a separate people from the nations if you intend to allow all nations to be a part of that people? Where's the sense in it? What might God intend to accomplish by extending the tent of Israel to encompass all nations?

The truly mysterious part of the Gentile inclusion is that it is at the very center of the Eternal Purpose of God. Let that ring in your head for a moment. The Eternal Purpose of God! Those are big words. Yet this is Paul's premise. The Gentile Inclusion, which constitutes the mystery of Messiah, is part of the Eternal Purpose of God. He explains it in verse 10 where he says, "[God's] intent was that now, through the Assembly (i.e. the body of believers in the Messiah), the manifold wisdom of God should be made known to the rulers and authorities in the heavenly realms."

What was God's intent in all of this? Through the mystery of the Gospel, God intends to bring the Gentiles into His people Israel.

His intent is that the manifold wisdom of God should be made known to the demonic rulers and authorities in heavenly realms.

When the LORD, through Messiah's blood, takes Gentile people away from their pagan gods, there is nothing the enemy can do about it. When God takes the children of clan Kelly away from the pagan gods of the Celts, when He takes the House of Lancaster away from the warrior gods of the Saxons, and when He redeems me and my family through Messiah, He is making a mockery of the demonic rulers and authorities of this world. Every Gentile who is taken from paganism, and joined to the people of Israel, represents a loss of territory and prestige for the Adversary. That is the manifold wisdom of God.

It is a plan of universal dominion, a plan by which God intends to take over the world. We Gentile believers are tokens of victory, God's victory in an ancient struggle against darkness. The Eternal Purpose of God is nothing less than the redemption of the whole world. And so we read, "His intent was that now, through the church, the manifold wisdom of God should be made known to the rulers and authorities in the heavenly realms, according to His Eternal Purpose which He accomplished in Messiah Yeshua our Lord" (Ephesians 3:10).

It is not unlike the passage from Deuteronomy (4:34–35) in which Moses reminds Israel of the supremacy of the LORD over all the other gods. He says to them, "Has any god ever tried to take for himself one nation out of another nation, by testings, by miraculous signs and wonders, by war, by a mighty hand and an outstretched arm, or by great and awesome deeds, like all the things the LORD your God did for you in Egypt before your very eyes? You were shown these things so that you might know that the LORD is God; besides Him there is no other." Through the act of taking the Israelites out of Egypt and away from Pharaoh and the other gods of Egypt, the LORD established His superiority over all those other gods. Israel was His trophy of victory. He used the Exodus from Egypt to establish His Name.

But the LORD was not about to stop with the redemption of Israel. The Exodus from Egypt set the pattern, but it was just the beginning. It foreshadowed a second Exodus, a greater Exodus, again effected by the blood of a lamb. This second Exodus is the mystery of Messiah, the redemption of the nations. It is as if God is repeating the Exodus from Egypt over and over again, and there is nothing Pharaoh or the gods of Egypt can do about it. The spiritual powers and principalities of the Gentile nations can only watch in dismay as their brickmakers join themselves to Israel and slip away through the Red Sea.

Our salvation is a demonstration of God's wisdom and sovereign power to rulers and authorities in the heavenly realms. Which of them, what other god, has ever tried to take for himself one nation out of every nation? Which god of the nations has done anything like it? Which god of the nations can do anything to stop it? The Eternal Purpose of God is nothing less than the salvation of the whole world.

The picture is much bigger than just me and my personal salvation. It is bigger than the liberation from Egypt. It is bigger than the salvation of Judah. It is bigger than the return of the Ten Lost Tribes. God's Eternal Purpose is that His wisdom should be made known to the rulers and authorities in heavenly realms by means of taking away their people, taking away their property, by means of redeeming a people out of every tribe, tongue and nation on earth.

That is the mystery of the Gospel for which Paul was willing to be held in chains.

Too Small a Thing

Isaiah spoke of this Mystery of Messiah.

In a vision recorded in his book of comfort, Isaiah saw the LORD speaking to His servant the Messiah. The LORD said to His servant, "It is too small a thing for you to be my servant to restore the tribes of Jacob and bring back those of Israel I have kept. I will also make you a light for the Gentiles, that you may bring my salvation to the ends of the earth."[7]

The scope of Messiah's work is not limited to the restoration of the tribes of Israel. That purpose is too small when compared with the greater purpose God has in mind. The Eternal Purpose of God is that Messiah should carry the LORD's salvation to the Gentiles, even to the ends of the earth. Notice that the prophet contrasts Gentiles with the tribes of Israel. They are not the same. The mission to restore the tribes of Israel is quite distinct from the salvation of the Gentiles.

The Gentiles of Isaiah 49 are the same Gentiles of the book of Ephesians. They are those strangers and aliens, those far off, strangers to the promises, without God and without hope. They are the foreskinned, the nations, the *ethnos*. They are the ones whom God intends to shine the light of Messiah upon. This is in keeping with His Eternal Purpose, that the manifold wisdom of God should be made known to the rulers and authorities in the heavenly realms. God's salvation must go to the ends of the earth. All nations will be blessed.

The Eternal Purpose of God culminates in a scene from the book of Revelation. John looks and sees "a great multitude, which no man could number, of all nations, and kindreds, and people, and tongues, [standing] before the throne, and before the Lamb."[8] This great, innumerable multitude is contrasted with the numerable 144,000 from the Twelve Tribes. The point of the passage is that God's salvation is universal and includes a Gentile majority from every ethnicity.

It's powerful, it's beautiful, and it is the very heart and mystery of the Gospel. It is in keeping with the Eternal Purpose of God.

The Israel of God

Therefore, we Gentiles have a legitimate place in Israel. We have a place more secure than any Jewish (or Israelite) ancestry, or spurious conversion ritual, could ever offer us. Our place is secured by the blood of Messiah and foreordained by the Eternal Purpose of God. We have an identity in Israel among the People of God. Just as Abraham believed by faith and it was credited to him as righteousness—before he was circumcised—we have a place in Israel.

Just as he brought near those who were far off, we have been brought near through Messiah and been given a place in Israel. Just as Ruth was compared to a goodly branch grafted into Abraham's tree, we have been grafted into Israel. Just as Joseph married Asenath, the pagan, Gentile daughter of an Egyptian priest, so too we have been granted a place in Israel by virtue of our Husband. Just as Jacob adopted Ephraim and Manasseh as his own, giving them a place among the tribes and the sons of Israel, so too our Father in heaven has adopted us into His people, along with His chosen people, the Hebrews. For we are all adopted children, and we have together been granted a place in Israel. Just as the Hebrews passed through the Red Sea like converts passing through an immersion, we have been born again. We are no longer slaves to sin. Rather, we have been born again of an imperishable seed. We are new creations, made a part of Israel. Just as the Master said, He has sheep not of the sheepfold of Israel which He must bring and join to that sheepfold; just so we have been brought in to Israel.

Just as Israel was betrothed by God to be His special treasure, a Kingdom of Priests and a Holy nation, so we have been joined to the bride and given a place in Israel.

Just as the voice of God at Sinai spoke in the languages of every nation and the Spirit spoke through the believers in the languages of every nation at Pentecost, we of every nation have a place in Israel. Just as Cornelius the Roman and his household received the Spirit prior to any conversion to Judaism, thereby demonstrating that salvation is by faith, we have a place in Israel.

Just as the Galatians and the Ephesians were made sons of Abraham by faith in the Seed of Abraham, we have a place in Israel. Just as John saw a mighty throng, a great multitude, which no man could number, of all nations, and kindreds, and people, and tongues standing before the Throne, we have a place in Israel.

ENDNOTES

1 Psalm 122:1–2

2 Josephus *Jewish War* 5:5:2

3 Josephus *Jewish Antiquities* 15:11:5

4 For example, compare the King James Version on the passage.

5 Paul's use of the Greek term "*dogma*" here implies that it is the Oral Tradition regarding Torah which is in view. *Dogma* is a mandate of a court of law, thus legislation of the sages. The sages' dogmatic interpretation of the Torah, during the days of Paul, created a sharp line of distinction between Jew and Gentile. It is this Torah based *dogma* which Messiah removes and abolishes, but God forbid that we should think Messiah abolished Torah.

6 Ezekiel 37

7 Isaiah 49:6

8 Revelation 7:9

Journey to Jerusalem

Epilogue

Journey to Jerusalem

The ancient prophets tell us that in the Messianic Age to come, we will find ourselves making pilgrimage to Jerusalem. In a sense, we are already on the journey.

To help guide us along the way, the prophets of Israel give us glimpses of our destination and destiny. According to the prophets, we are going to Messianic Jerusalem. We are going up to the City of the Great King.

Keeping this goal in clear view makes it easier to understand the journey. Our final destination is Jerusalem and the service of the King. There are some of us who are the descendents of Abraham, whether ethnically or through absorption into the Jewish community. This is our journey. There are also some (many) of us who are not part of the ethnic or social family of Abraham. We, Gentiles, hail from all nations, and we have also been privileged to join this great pilgrimage. Abraham is our father too, albeit by faith only. This is our journey too. Together, we are all on the same road. We are all heading toward the same city to worship and serve the same King. According to the prophets, the picture is not complete without both of us.

Isaiah Sees the Future

The prophet Isaiah paints an especially vivid picture of our pilgrimage. He saw all nations making pilgrimage to Jerusalem. He tells us that in the Messianic Age, the Temple in Jerusalem will be the "chief" place of worship. All nations will ascend to it. In Jerusalem, all nations will learn the ways of Torah. The result will be universal peace.

> In the last days the mountain of the LORD's Temple will be established as chief among the mountains; it will be raised above the hills, and all nations will stream to it.

> Many peoples will come and say, "Come, let us go up to the mountain of the LORD, to the house of the God of Jacob. He will teach us his ways, so that we may walk in his paths." The law will go out from Zion, the word of the LORD from Jerusalem. He will judge between the nations and will settle disputes for many peoples. They will beat their swords into plowshares and their spears into pruning hooks. Nation will not take up sword against nation, nor will they train for war anymore. (Isaiah 2:2–4)

Isaiah tells us that God intends to bring all peoples into His Kingdom. Messiah Himself will be like "a banner for the peoples, the nations will rally to him, and his place of rest will be glorious…"[1] His place of rest is Messianic Jerusalem.

Through the prophet Isaiah, the Spirit of Messiah declares, "The Torah will go out from me; my justice will become a light to the nations… my arm will bring justice to the nations…"[2] Isaiah tells us that the nations will keep the Sabbath. The nations will keep the covenant of Torah. Their burnt offerings and sacrifices will be accepted on the LORD's altar. The Temple in Jerusalem "will be called a house of prayer for all nations."[3] As the nations ascend to Jerusalem, they will bring the exiles of Israel with them.[4] Together, Jew and Gentile will worship before the LORD on the monthly New Moons and the weekly Sabbaths.

"'From one New Moon to another and from one Sabbath to another, all mankind will come and bow down before me,' says the LORD" (Isaiah 66:23).

All peoples, all mankind, will be keeping the New Moons and the weekly Sabbath. Observing the New Moons means they will keep the biblical calendar. Observing the weekly Sabbath means they keep the covenant sign of Israel.[5]

Peeking at the Kingdom

The mystery of the Gospel is the inclusion of the Gentiles into the People of God, the grafting into Israel. The Eternal Purpose of God is nothing less than the redemption of the whole creation. Messiah accomplishes both. In the Messianic Age to come, He will subdue all nations and make all mankind subject to the good and perfect Law of God. Messiah's kingdom is the destination of the journey.

As the prophet Isaiah described the great pilgrimage ascending to Messianic Jerusalem, he saw that the pilgrims were not just Israelites. Among the multitudes ascending to the Holy City, he saw strangers, foreigners and people of other nations. He cried out to Jerusalem, "Nations will come to your light, and kings to the brightness of your dawn. Lift up your eyes and look about you: All assemble and come to you; your sons come from afar, and your daughters are carried on the arm."[6]

And as the rivers of pilgrims from every tribe, tongue and nation on earth approach the Holy City, Isaiah cried out to them, "Pass through, pass through the gates! Prepare the way for the people. Build up, build up the highway! Remove the stones. Raise a banner for the nations..."[7] He welcomes the pilgrims into the Gates of Jerusalem.

The Road to Jerusalem

The picture is clear. All nations will ascend to Jerusalem to worship the King, learn His Law (Torah), and keep His commandments. Messianic Jerusalem is the destination. In that day, the whole world will be keeping the Torah. All nations will make pilgrimage to Jerusalem because Jerusalem will be the capital city of all nations. The kingdom of Israel will be universal. All men will serve the King of Israel according to the Torah of Israel. That is the destination; that is the goal.

Knowing that we will all be keeping the biblical calendar in Messiah's Kingdom makes it clear that keeping the calendar is part of Kingdom living. In that day, all mankind will keep the Seventh Day, biblical Sabbath. When we sit down to eat with the Master, the menu options will certainly not include shrimp cocktail or baked ham.

We would do well to let the rule of the coming Kingdom dictate how the servants of the King live now. In that day, all nations will keep Torah. The Torah shall go forth from Zion, a light to all nations and a law to all men. If the Torah is the law of the Kingdom, shouldn't all the subjects of the King obey that law? If Messianic Jerusalem is our final destination, shouldn't we turn our hearts toward her now? We don't have to wait until we arrive in her gates; we can begin the celebration right now.

After all, the message of Yeshua was simply this: "Repent! Turn! The Kingdom of Heaven is now!"[8]

ENDNOTES

1 Isaiah 11:10–12

2 Isaiah 51:4–5

3 Isaiah 56:1–7

4 Isaiah 62:10–20

5 Exodus 31:17

6 Isaiah 60:3–4

7 Isaiah 62:10

8 Matthew 4:17

Appendix

Appendix
The Soreg

In the course of his massive remodeling of the Jerusalem Temple, King Herod extended the Temple Mount significantly by constructing a retaining wall and adding fill.

Prior to Herod's additions, the original Temple Mount platform was marked off by a balustrade of stone latticework (*soreg*). The balustrade was designed to maintain the original dimensions of the Temple area—and to keep non-Jews out. Second Temple Judaism regarded that original area as sacrosanct to Jews alone.

The *Mishnah*, in *Middot* 2:3, reports the *soreg* as 10 handbreadths high. Josephus recalls it as a slightly taller 3 cubits. So it was approximately four feet in height. The courtyard outside of this barrier was referred to as the Court of the Gentiles. Plaques were posted on the balustrade forbidding Gentiles to go beyond it. Josephus, an eye-witness to the Temple, describes the barrier as follows:

> There was a partition made of stone all around, whose height was three cubits; its construction was very elegant; upon it stood pillars, at equal distances from one another, declaring the law of purity, some in Greek, and some in Roman letters, that "no foreigner should go within that sanctuary." (*Jewish War* 5:5:2)

> Thus was the first enclosure. In the midst of which, and not far from it, was the second, to be gone up to by a few steps: this was encompassed by a stone wall for a partition, with an inscription, which forbade any foreigner to go in under pain of death. (*Antiquities* 15:11:5)

Up until the late 19th century, this dividing wall was known to us only from the ancient sources mentioned above. Then, during Clermont and Ganneau's 1871 excavations of Jerusalem, a stone plaque was discovered. It apparently came from the original dividing wall and bears the complete Greek text. The plaque now resides in the Istanbul Museum.

The inscription reads: "No foreigner is to enter within the balustrade and enclosure around the Temple area. Whoever is caught will have himself to blame for his death which will follow." Incredibly, in 1936, another such inscription was unearthed near Jerusalem's Lion Gate. The second inscription was only partially preserved. Both inscriptions are pictured here.

(Photos from JUC field book, Istanbul Museum, and Israel Museum, respectively. No credits given.)

```
ΜΗΘΕΝΑ ΑΛΛΟΓΕΝΗΕΙΣΠΟ
ΡΕΥΕΣΟΛΙΕΝΤΟΣΤΟΙΠΕ
ΡΙΤΟΙΕΡΟΝΤΡΥΦΑΚΤΟΥΚΑΙ
ΠΕΡΙΒΟΛΟΥΟΣ ΔΑΝΛΗ
ΦΘΗΕΑΥΤΩΙΑΙΤΙΟΣΕ Σ
ΤΑΙΔΙΑΤΟΕ Ξ ΛΚΟΛΟΥ
ΟΕΙΝΟΑΝΑΤΟΝ
```

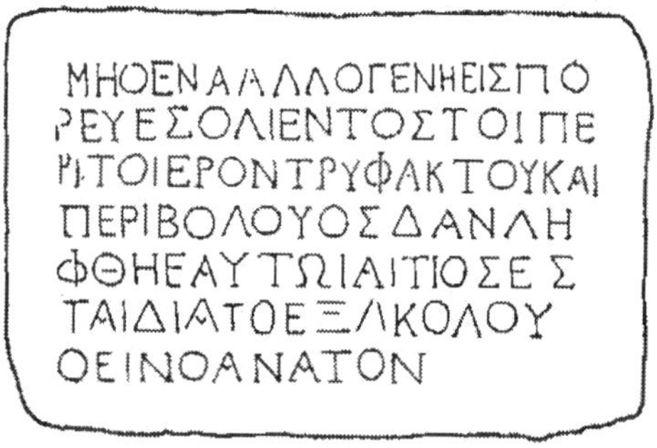

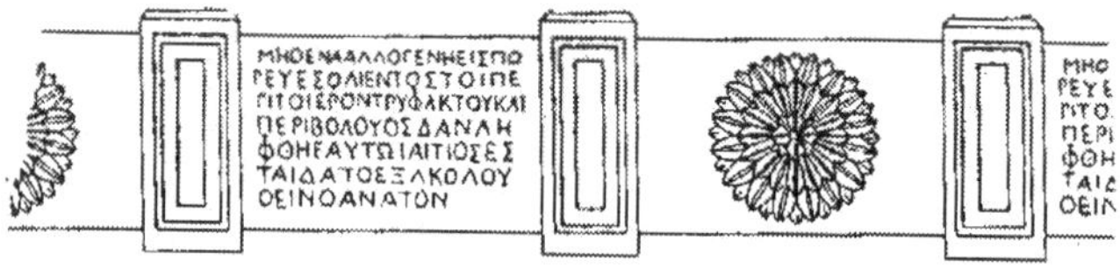

No foreigner is to enter within the balustrade and enclosure around the temple area. Whoever is caught will have himself to blame for his death which will follow.

Bibliography

Bibliography

Attridge, Harold W. and Gohei, Hata, eds. 1992. *Eusebius, Christianity, and Judaism*. Detroit, MI. Wayne State University Press.

Berkowitz, Ariel and D'vorah. 1999. *Take Hold*. First Fruits of Zion. USA and Israel.

Berkowitz, Ariel and D'vorah. 1996. *Torah Rediscovered*. First Fruits of Zion. USA and Israel.

Bruce, F.F. 1988. *The Book of Acts*. Grand Rapids, MI. Wm. B. Eerdmans Publishing Co.

Charlesworth, James H. 1983. *The Old Testament Pseudipigrapha*. 2 vols. Doubleday, New York.

Chasidah, Yishai. 1994. *Encyclopedia of Biblical Personalities*. Jerusalem: Shaar Press.

Daube, David. 1956. *The New Testament and Rabbinic Judaism*. University of London, The Athlone Press. Great Britain.

Gaston, Lloyd. 1987. *Paul and the Torah*. University of British Columbia Press. Vancouver, Canada.

Hegg, Tim. 2002. *The Letter Writer: Paul's Background and Torah Perspective*. First Fruits of Zion. USA and Israel.

Hegg, Tim. 2003. *It is Often Said: Comments and Comparisons of Evangelical Thought & Hebraic Theology*. 2 Vols. First Fruits of Zion. USA and Israel.

Hegg, Tim. 2003. "The Torah is Only for Jews". Two parts. *Bikurei Tziyon* #77, #78.

Kaplan, Aryeh. 1995. *The Aryeh Kaplan Anthology, Vol. 2* (Waters of Eden). Brooklyn New York. Mesorah Publications, Ltd.

Kling, Simcha. 1987. *Embracing Judaism*. New York. The Rabbinical Assembly.

Lachs, Samuel Tobias. 1987. *A Rabbinic Commentary on the New Testament*. Hoboken, NJ. Ktav Publishing House, Inc.

Metford, J.C.J. 1983. *Dictionary of Christian Lore and Legend*. London, England. Thames and Hudson.

Patai, Raphael. 1988. *The Messiah Texts*. Detroit, MI. Wayne State University Press.

Whiston, William. 1999. *The New Complete Works of Josephus*. Grand Rapids, MI. Kregel Publications.

Williamson, G. A. 1965. *Eusebius: The History of the Church*. Mpls, MN. Augsburg Publishing.

Scherman, Nosson, ed. and trans. 1994. *The Stone Edition Chumash*. Brooklyn, NY. Mesorah Publications Ltd.

Scherman, Nosson, ed. and trans. 1986. *Bereishis*. Brooklyn, NY. Mesorah Publications Ltd.

Young, Brad. 1995. *Jesus the Jewish Theologian*. Hendrickson Publishers. Peabody, MA.

Young, Brad. 1998. *The Parables*. Jewish Tradition and Christian Interpretation. Hendrickson Publishers. Peabody, MA.

The Soncino Talmud. Brooklyn, NY. Judaica Press.

The Soncino Midrash Rabbah. Brooklyn, NY. Judaica Press.

The New International Version of the Bible. Zondervan.

Scripture Index

Scripture Index

1 Peter

Revelation

Additional Books

FellowHeirs

Jews and Gentiles Together in the Family of God.

Tim Hegg. FellowHeirs takes on the difficult question of the Gentile believer's relationship to Torah. Guaranteed to rock many theological boats inside and outside of the Hebrew Roots movement, FellowHeirs is a must read for every serious student of the Bible.

Paperback | $13.97

The Letter Writer

Paul's Background and Torah Perspective

Tim Hegg. Has the Body of Messiah missed significant blessing found in the Torah resulting from a skewed perception and misunderstanding of Paul and his writings? It is time for us to take a new and honest look at Paul as an apostle who was Torah observant, faithful to the call of Israel, and a great man that encouraged the followers of the Messiah to embrace the teachings of Moses and with great passion declared Yeshua to be the Messiah of Israel!

The Letter Writer challenges traditional Christian viewpoints of the Apostle Paul, his message and the foundation of his theological approach and understanding. Through this remarkable book Tim Hegg attempts to re-establish a biblical, historical, and cultural understanding of Paul—the Torah observant Apostle.

Paperback | $18.97

Torah Rediscovered

Challenging Centuries of Misinterpretation and Neglect

Ariel and D'vorah Berkowitz. The Berkowitz's instant classic Torah Rediscovered is back in print, newly revised and updated. A delightful introduction to the Torah and the world of Torah thought, this is one of the pioneering works that opened the case for Torah observance among believers. Separating Torah from legalism and grace from lawlessness, the name says it all; this is "Torah Rediscovered."

Paperback | $14.97

The Mystery of the Gospel

Jews, Gentiles and the Eternal Purpose of God

D. Thomas Lancaster. In a friendly narrative style, Lancaster works backwards through Paul's rabbinic scholarship to unravel the deep Mystery of the Gospel—Gentile participation in Israel. This book offers a gentle answer to the Two-House movement and a breathtaking journey through the scriptures.

Paperback | $14.97

Audio Book | 6 CDs and Case | $49.97

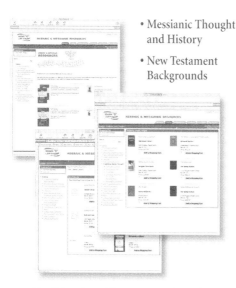

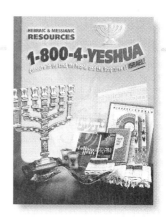

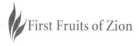

Torah Discipleship